CONSTELLATIONS

Like the future itself, the imaginative possibilities of science fiction are limitless. And the very development of cinema is inextricably linked to the genre, which, from the earliest depictions of space travel and the robots of silent cinema to the immersive 3D wonders of contemporary blockbusters, has continually pushed at the boundaries. **Constellations** provides a unique opportunity for writers to share their passion for science fiction cinema in a book-length format, each title devoted to a significant film from the genre. Writers place their chosen film in a variety of contexts – generic, institutional, social, historical – enabling **Constellations** to map the terrain of science fiction cinema from the past to the present… and the future.

'This stunning, sharp series of books fills a real need for authoritative, compact studies of key science fiction films. Written in a direct and accessible style by some of the top critics in the field, brilliantly designed, lavishly illustrated and set in a very modern typeface that really shows off the text to best advantage, the volumes in the **Constellations** series promise to set the standard for SF film studies in the 21st century.'
Wheeler Winston Dixon, Ryan Professor of Film Studies, University of Nebraska

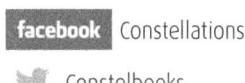
Constellations

Constelbooks

Also available in this series

12 Monkeys Susanne Kord

Aliens Cristina Massaccesi

Blade Runner Sean Redmond

Brainstorm Joseph Maddrey

Children of Men Dan Dinello

Close Encounters of the Third Kind Jon Towlson

The Damned Nick Riddle

Dune Christian McCrea

Ex Machina Joshua Grimm

Inception David Carter

Jurassic Park Paul Bullock

Lost Brigid Cherry

Mad Max Martyn Conterio

Minority Report D. Harlan Wilson

Moon Brian J Robb

The OA David Sweeney

RoboCop Omar Ahmed

Rollerball Andrew Nette

Seconds Jez Conolly & Emma Westwood

Stalker Jon Hoel

The Stepford Wives Samantha Lindop

CONSTELLATIONS

Ghidorah, the Three-Headed Monster

Christopher Stewardson

Acknowledgements

Firstly, I owe an enormous debt of gratitude to John Atkinson, Ally Lee, and Christabel Scaife at Auteur Publishing and Liverpool University Press for getting this project off the ground and for shepherding it to the finish line – and for patiently answering many anxious questions along the way! Thank you to Laura Mee and Craig Ian Mann for their encouragement, kindness, and invaluable feedback.

A special thanks to Mariko and Ed Godziszewski, not only for translating innumerable Japanese texts but also for offering sources and ideas. Their immense generosity and faith in this book have meant a great deal. Thank you to Toyomi Togo (東郷登代美) for her permission to use original drawings by Yasuyuki Inoue (井上泰幸); and thank you to Oki Miyano for facilitating our conversations and for offering expertise and insight. Thank you to Hannah and Michiko Green for their help with further translations and useful feedback – and importantly for their friendship. Thank you to Hayley Scanlon for their kind help and patience with additional translations. I'd also like to thank Tom Filden of Nichiei Partners (yaku.co) for their translations and research of other Japanese sources.

Thank you to Daisuke Miyao, Yoshikuni Igarashi, Pauline Charlotte, Sydney Perkins, Cody Himes, and Josh Naugh, whose invaluable feedback, generosity with resources, and reassurances have immeasurably improved my arguments. Thank you to Steve Ryfle, Patrick Galvan, and Erik Homenick for their helpful conversations, suggestions, and encouragement. It has all meant a great deal.

A very special thank you as well to Hamish Steele for producing the original piece on this book's cover.

Thank you to my partner, Tilly, for their love and enthusiasm. Thank you for listening to my ideas late at night and for being my rock when I was hit with doubts. Sharing films with you is always a joy.

Finally, thank you to my parents for their encouragement and belief – and for showing me *Son of Godzilla* on VHS when I was seven.

First published in 2025 by Liverpool University Press
Liverpool University Press, 4 Cambridge Street, Liverpool L69 7ZU
www.liverpooluniversitypress.co.uk
Copyright © Christopher Stewardson 2025

Series design: Nikki Hamlett at Cassels Design
Set by Cassels Design, Luton, UK.

All rights reserved. No part of this publication may be reproduced in any material form (including photocopying or storing in any medium by electronic means and whether or not transiently or incidentally to some other use of this publication) without the permission of the copyright owner.

British Library Cataloguing-in-Publication Data
A catalogue record for this book is available from the British Library

ISBN paperback: 9781836243885
ISBN hardback: 9781836243878
eISBN (PDF): 9781836244066
eISBN (ePub): 9781836243779

Contents

Acknowledgements ....

Introduction 7

Chapter 1: Godzilla by 1964 11

Chapter 2: The Making of *Ghidorah, the Three-Headed Monster* 39

Chapter 3: Interpreting *Ghidorah, the Three-Headed Monster* 63

Chapter 4: The US Release of *Ghidorah, the Three-Headed Monster* 89

Chapter 5: The Legacy of *Ghidorah, the Three-Headed Monster* 115

Bibliography 139

Index 149

Introduction

Ghidorah, the Three-Headed Monster (1964, Ishiro Honda) is a significant entry in Toho's Godzilla franchise. The film introduced one of the series' most popular characters in King Ghidorah; it consolidated the relationship between prior Toho special effects films and developed ideas from previous narratives; and it decisively altered Godzilla's characterisation. The film's release in December 1964 grants it specific relevance. *Ghidorah* appeared less than two months after the 1964 Tokyo Olympics, an event which drew global attention to new and highly curated images of Japan in the post-war arena. In turn, this highlights how changes to Godzilla – both as a character and a film series – can be situated within these shifting national narratives.

This book aims to explore *Ghidorah, the Three-Headed Monster* in depth. We shall begin with a brief overview of Japan's history from the Meiji Restoration to the aftermath of World War II to observe its reflections in the Godzilla series, identifying both continuity and change. While the 1964 Tokyo Olympics consciously signposted a curated transformation from imperial aggressor to prosperous, democratic nation, closer scrutiny raises questions over the veracity of Japan's new image. Numerous figures integral to Japan's imperial aggression were intimately involved in the country's recovery, systems of power also remained, and the ideological aims of the United States proved highly influential. Understanding this history is paramount for a recollection of Japan's post-war evolution, and how that evolution touched the Godzilla series.

We shall also chronicle *Ghidorah*'s production, examining the content of its early script drafts, its cast members, and the work of its special effects technicians.

Our third chapter offers an interpretation of *Ghidorah*'s themes and ideas. Ten years on from the original *Godzilla* (1954, Ishiro Honda), *Ghidorah* introduces a friendlier version of the monster. Placing the original, black-and-white *Godzilla* – made two years after the US Occupation's official end and brimming with anxious dread – next to the colourful *Ghidorah* makes the film's historical reflections clear: the new, heroic Godzilla parallels a rehabilitated Japan in 1964. We shall therefore contrast that character evolution with the political function of the Tokyo Olympics. This chapter will also look at thematic continuities between *Ghidorah* and prior Toho films, viewing the film as the culmination of a loose trilogy with *Mothra* (1961, Ishiro Honda) and *Mothra vs. Godzilla* (1964, Ishiro Honda).

Chapter Four will introduce and contextualise the film's 1965 US release. The first Godzilla films to arrive in America did so via extensive alteration and can be understood as separate entities to their original Japanese counterparts. The reasons behind the localisation process touch everything from Hollywood hegemony and the American art-film market to trends in the Japanese film industry. We shall discuss the changes made to *Ghidorah* via localisation, as well as the film's critical reception in the US.

Finally, in Chapter Five, we shall look at *Ghidorah*'s legacy. We will inspect how King Ghidorah has reappeared in the Godzilla series with an eye toward the character's symbolic potential. We will also examine *Ghidorah*'s consolidation of narrative connections between various Toho science-fiction titles, and how Godzilla's character shift interacts with audience perception and relation to the monster.

It is hoped that this book can be a useful contribution to the ongoing scholarship on the Godzilla series. Authors such as Yoshikuni Igarashi, Takayuki Tatsumi, Inuhiko Yomota, Nobutaka Suzuki, Masumi Kaneda, Steve Ryfle, and Ed Godziszewski have written about these films in a variety of ways, from in-depth examinations of their production histories to insightful analyses of their sociopolitical underpinnings. It is on the foundation of their work that this book is possible.

Notes on Titles

We shall refer to the film in question as *Ghidorah, the Three-Headed Monster*. As with many Godzilla films, the picture has gone by several titles. For example, the original Japanese title from 1964, *San Daikaiju Chikyu Saidai no Kessen*, translates to *Three Giant Monsters: The Greatest Battle on Earth*. This was then altered to *Godzilla, Mothra, King Ghidorah: The Greatest Battle on Earth* for the film's 1971 Champion Festival reissue. When released in the US in 1965, the film was called *Ghidrah, the*

Three-Headed Monster. There are also at least two international titles given by Toho. The first is *Monster of Monsters: Ghidorah*, which is listed in Toho Films Vol. 10 (a catalogue used to sell Toho's titles overseas) and elsewhere. The second is *Ghidorah: The Three-Headed Monster*, which may have been adopted as an English title in the early 1970s and is featured on an English-language poster prepared by Toho. For reader familiarity, we shall refer to the film as *Ghidorah, the Three-Headed Monster* unless otherwise noted.

Synopsis

Ghidorah, the Three-Headed Monster begins with reporter Naoko (Yuriko Hoshi) interviewing a UFO club, the leader of which warns that Earth is out of balance. A meteorite shower suddenly begins and one crashes near Kurobe Dam. At the same time, Princess Salno (Akiko Wakabayashi) is flying to Japan from the fictional nation of Selgina. A bright light appears telling her to stand up and leave the plane just before it explodes mid-air.

Naoko's brother, Detective Shindo (Yosuke Natsuki), was assigned to guard the Princess before her apparent assassination, and he is naturally shocked when she appears in Japan professing to come from Venus. She warns of great calamities, including the return of Godzilla and Rodan. Salno's would-be assassins (agents of a political enemy from Selgina) also arrive in Japan to finish the job. Meanwhile, a Professor Murai (Hiroshi Koizumi) investigates the crashed meteorite, finding strange magnetic properties.

Naoko believes this supposed prophetess is the perfect subject for a new series run by her publication and seeks her out. She briefly clashes with her brother, who is trying to confirm whether this mysterious woman is indeed the Princess. The assassins attempt to kill the Princess for a second time, but she is saved by Shindo and the intervention of the Shobijin (Emi and Yumi Ito), Mothra's twin fairies from Infant Island.

Just as the Princess warned, Rodan and Godzilla return and rampage across Japan. Meanwhile, the Princess is taken for treatment with Dr. Tsukamoto (Takashi Shimura).

CONSTELLATIONS

Under hypnosis, she reveals that all life on Venus was destroyed centuries ago by King Ghidorah, a powerful monster that has arrived on Earth – it eventually erupts from the crashed meteorite. The Shobijin suggest that Mothra could convince Godzilla and Rodan to unite against King Ghidorah.

The assassins make another attempt on the Princess' life at Tsukamoto's clinic, planning to sabotage her shock treatment. Godzilla and Rodan inadvertently thwart their plans when they destroy nearby power lines, and a brief firefight ensues between Shindo and the assassins.

Mothra arrives in Japan and heads to Mount Fuji where Godzilla and Rodan are fighting. Naoko, Detective Shindo, Professor Murai, the Princess, Dr. Tsukamoto, and the Shobijin watch as Mothra communicates with the two monsters. The Shobijin translate the conversation, revealing that Godzilla and Rodan refuse to fight King Ghidorah because mankind hates them. At the same time, King Ghidorah approaches Mount Fuji, killing most of the assassins in the process.

With her efforts unsuccessful, Mothra goes to fight King Ghidorah on her own. However, Godzilla and Rodan eventually join the battle. During the conflict, the Princess wanders to a nearby gorge to contact an unnamed deity. The final assassin, Malmess (Hisaya Ito), tries to shoot her but Shindo intervenes again. The Princess is grazed by a bullet and suddenly regains her senses, recognising Malmess and calling him a traitor. Before Malmess can finally kill her, an avalanche of boulders crushes him. Godzilla, Rodan, and Mothra defeat King Ghidorah, who retreats into space.

With all crises resolved, Princess Salno returns to her home country. Before leaving, she bids a tearful farewell to Shindo. The Shobijin and Mothra similarly depart for Infant Island, saying goodbye to Godzilla and Rodan.

Chapter One: Godzilla by 1964

The first ten years of the Godzilla series witnessed changes in tone, focus, and presentation. Indeed, by 1964, it was a *series*, with five entries to its name. Its developments since 1954 reflect similar image transformations in post-war Japan, and it is therefore necessary to provide a historical background to contextualise how and when *Ghidorah, the Three-Headed Monster* was produced. As facets of Japan's post-war history are observable throughout the Godzilla series, a brief, non-exhaustive historical foundation will therefore ground later discussions.

We will similarly explore Toho's other special effects films released between 1954 and 1964. These films shared many of the same creative and technical staff members, as well as similar thematic discussions. It is therefore useful to touch upon their place within this filmography. Some of these films will be discussed in more depth than others due to the wide breadth of the subject.

Imperial Japan

Following the 1868 Meiji Restoration, which restored rule to the emperor, Japan was reconfigured and reconceptualised as a nation state. Its borders, both internal and external, were reimagined and reasserted. In the case of the latter, these assertions manifested in violent colonial expansion. The Ryukyu Kingdom, for example, which had been held under a specific subordinate relationship to Japan since 1609, became fully absorbed within the Japanese nation state as Okinawa prefecture, annexed by 1879 (Matsumura, 2015, 26–48; Uemura, 2003, 107–23). To the north, settler colonisation similarly consolidated Japan's control and formulation of Hokkaido, further subjugating the Ainu (Lu, 2019, 39–41). On the world stage, Japan asserted its imperial power via the First Sino-Japanese War (1894–95) and the Russo-Japanese War (1904–05), bringing further territories in the process, including Taiwan, Korea, and parts of Manchuria; Korea was fully annexed by 1910 (Bailey, 1996, 12; Harding, 2019, 160–63).

This mass expansion initially secured a sense of parity with the Western imperial powers, in whose image Japan's ambitions were partly modelled. However, this soon gave way to Western unease at what they saw as a Pacific rival.

By the early 1930s, Japan's militarists were calling for further expansion in China, and so the Kwantung Army based in Manchuria instigated episodes of violence which were blamed on the Chinese and used to justify further mobilisation – all lauded in Japanese newspapers back home (McClain, 2001, 410). The puppet state of Manchukuo was installed in March 1932.

Imperial Japan, via Chief Delegate Yosuke Matsuoka, defended its actions to the League of Nations, speaking of China in belittling, racist terms as a backwards country in dire condition, and positioning Japan as a benevolent neighbour passing on its enlightenment (Matsuoka, 1933, 7). After Japan's defence was rejected, Emperor Hirohito issued an edict announcing the nation's withdrawal from the League in March 1933 (McClain, 2001, 416–19).

Japan launched its full-scale invasion of China in 1937, initiating the Second Sino-Japanese War. Imperial Japan inflicted genocidal brutality on cities like Nanjing, subjecting its population to a weeks-long campaign of rape, arson, mass execution, and sadism. Historians estimate that 300,000 people were killed, and similar atrocities were committed against further conquered territories (Harding, 2019, 195). By the war's end, 15 million Chinese had been killed (Dower, 2000, 22).

Japan's expansion in East and Southeast Asia, under the doctrine of the so-called Greater East-Asia Co-Prosperity Sphere (which sought to "unite" these regions under Imperial Japanese military and economic domination), led the US to enact resource embargos on materials like gasoline. Further items like scrap iron were similarly prohibited when Japan signed the Tripartite Pact with Nazi Germany and Fascist Italy in September 1940. Moreover, when Japan moved further into French Indochina in July 1941, the US froze Japanese assets in America and enforced a further embargo on all oil exports to Japan (McClain, 2001, 474–76).

For the remainder of that year, multiple proposals were sent between Japan and America, with the former seeking recognition of its territorial conquests, and the latter trying to keep its regional financial interests safe (Melber, 2021, 47–48). After further attempts at negotiation failed, an Imperial conference ratified Japan's decision to go to war. On 7 December 1941, Imperial Japan attacked the American naval base at Pearl Harbor, thrusting the nation into direct conflict with the US and its allies.

Japan in the Second World War

Following the attack on Pearl Harbor, Japan quickly overran further territories including Hong Kong, Malaya, Singapore, and Burma (Bailey, 1996, 19). However, as John Dower (2000, 22) notes, Japan had "run amok, badly miscalculating both the resilience of the Chinese resistance and the resources, psychological as well as material, that the United States could bring to a protracted conflict". Japan quickly found itself struggling for resources, and the so-called "victory disease" of its initial efforts was short-lived.

In the United States, Executive Order 9066 was signed in 1942, initiating the imprisonment of around 120,000 Japanese Americans (as well as Japanese nationals deported to the US from other countries including Canada, Panama, Peru, Mexico, and elsewhere) in concentration camps, most of which were along the West Coast. The accusations of disloyalty used to justify this act of mass violence were rooted in anti-Japanese racism, which similarly ran rampant via wartime propaganda (Weglyn, 2003, 28–74).

In March 1945, 334 American B-29s carrying oil, phosphorous, jellied gasoline, and napalm decimated Tokyo in a firebomb raid. Up to 100,000 people perished as the city burned, with one-fifth of the city's industrial sites wiped out in a single night (McClain, 2001, 506). A similar fate awaited the cities of Osaka, Kobe, and Nagoya.

Then, on 6 August 1945, the world changed forever. The United States deployed a weapon of incomparable scale and ferocious cruelty. *Little Boy*, a 15-kiloton uranium bomb, was dropped over the city of Hiroshima; 140,000 people were killed that day or would die from their injuries by the end of 1945 (Southard, 2016, 30). Three days later, a 22-kiloton plutonium bomb named *Fat Man* exploded over Nagasaki. Another 60,000 to 70,000 people were killed on 9 August alone (Southard, 2016, 41–42; McClain, 2001, 514).

In the intervening days, the Soviet Union had declared war on Japan and had entered

Manchuria. Defeat, as Japan's leaders had been acutely aware, was inevitable. On 15 August 1945, a broadcast was transmitted from Emperor Hirohito himself. He called upon the nation to "endure the unendurable". The war was over. Japan had surrendered.

The US Occupation

By the war's end, Japan was devastated, having lost close to three million people (Dower, 2000, 22). Its cities lay in ruins and nine million Japanese were displaced or homeless (Harding, 2019, 229). Poverty, disease, and malnutrition were widespread, with Japanese civilians suffering a 17% reduction in daily calory intake per person since 1941, compared to reductions of 2% in Britain (Bailey, 1996, 23). It would take years for thousands of Japanese troops to be repatriated, scattered as they were in occupied territories or under Allied capture.

When the Americans arrived two weeks after Hirohito's 15 August address, they were met with a country decimated beyond expectation. As Dower (2000, 44) notes, "Japan at the war's end was vastly weaker than anyone outside the country had imagined – or anyone inside it had acknowledged".

On paper, the occupation of Japan was to be a joint Allied operation, but its implementation quickly proved otherwise. The US and the Supreme Command of the Allied Powers (SCAP), headed by General Douglas MacArthur, ensured that the official arms of Allied oversight were reduced to simply rubber-stamping policies – thanks to a clause which required unanimity for decisions (Sims, 2001, 242).

Without delay, SCAP set about its mission of demilitarisation, democratisation, and decentralisation. Its first major directives came in October 1945: all political prisoners were to be released, the Peace Preservation Law (which had effectively criminalised membership of the communist party via imprisonment and death sentences for anyone found guilty of aiming to overthrow the system of private property or the *kokutai*, the "national body") was to be revoked, women were to be enfranchised, education was to be liberalised, and the economy would be decentralised (Sims, 2001, 239). Japan's army and navy were also abolished (McClain, 2001, 534).

Ghidorah, the Three-Headed Monster

Beginning in 1946, SCAP began purging militarists and wartime leaders from public office, though this would prove only temporary. The purge was far-reaching. Dozens of Japan's film-studio bosses found themselves briefly removed for having collaborated with the Imperial government in the production of propaganda films, including Daiei's Masaichi Nagata, who would go on to produce its early Gamera films. Eiji Tsuburaya, *Godzilla*'s special effects director, was similarly blacklisted for a time because of his convincing filmed recreations of Japanese war exploits.

Discussions were held over the fate of the Emperor and whether he would be tried as a war criminal. On the contrary, retaining the emperor served many purposes for the US and Japan's elites, illuminating how continuities from Imperial Japan were an immediate part of the post-war reconfiguration. On its surface, MacArthur and the US believed that maintaining the emperor system would promote domestic stability (Sims, 2001, 243). More pressingly, its preservation allowed the US to maintain their dominant control over Occupation reform, leveraging Hirohito's escape from prosecution to encourage Japanese acceptance of their terms for a new constitution. If Japan was unwilling to accept the draft constitution proposals prepared by the US, the Emperor's survival – and therefore the future of the Imperial institution itself – could not be guaranteed. Moreover, MacArthur made it known that he was not above putting constitutional reform to the public, effectively threatening the position of the governing elites. And if *their* position was maintained, the US could rely on mutually beneficial co-operation to enact its reforms through an intact system. The new constitution could then be legitimised via the Imperial institution (Marotti, 2013, 39–40).

The Emperor's survival also played its role in what Yoshikuni Igarashi describes as the foundational narrative of post-war Japan. The Emperor's 15 August address was the first time Hirohito's voice had been heard on the radio, and it had been to announce the war's end, beginning the association of Hirohito as peacemaker. His rescript had also presented a dehistoricised narrative of the war, defining the conflict as lasting almost four years and therefore leaving out Japan's preceding colonial violence. It subsequently mentioned the "long road" ahead and "construction for the future", immediately pivoting away from the implicit questions of responsibility. The arms of the Occupation would also disperse a complementary narrative that ascribed war responsibility to a small but powerful group of militarists, helping to exonerate the Emperor – and therefore the people, since they had fought in his name – and detaching Japan's war machine from the imperialism of the nineteenth and early twentieth centuries that had helped pave the way for the conditions of 1945. The processes of curated conversion from enemy to ally, past to present, were moving quickly (Igarashi, 2000, 26–27; Harding, 2019, 248).

Taking effect on 3 May 1947, Japan's new constitution was deceptively striking in its details, and in its distinctions from the US constitution on which it was based. Article 1 identified the emperor as the head of state, "deriving his position from the will of the people with whom resides sovereign power" (Kingston, 2014, 119). Article 9 stripped Japan of its ability to wage war, stating that land, sea, and air forces would never be maintained. Notably, Article 28 guaranteed the right of workers to organise, bargain, and act collectively.

Running counter to the constitution's protections for freedom of speech (Article 21), the Civil Censorship Detachment (CCD) monitored print, film, media, radio, personal mail, and telephone and telegraph communications between 1945 and 1949. The CCD enforced a list of banned topics, including obvious targets like anti-American sentiments, but also: discussion of the difference in living standards between the Japanese and the Occupation forces; the "fraternisation" between the Japanese and US servicemen; and references to food shortages (Southard, 2016, 145–46). Criticism of the Emperor was permitted, but only insofar as it did not criticise or question the Occupation in the process, since the two were deeply intwined (Hirano, 1992, 111–12). Also at work was the Civil Information and Education Section (CIE), which ensured Japanese filmmakers pursued the principles of Occupation reform. Scripts were sent to the CIE during pre-production and all completed films were similarly submitted to secure a seal of approval – a necessity for release (Anderson & Richie, 1982, 162; Hirano, 1992, 6). CIE's post-production censorship continued until 1952.

Emperor Hirohito's function for the Occupation intersected with these structures in 1946 via Fumio Kamei's *Tragedy of Japan*, a documentary which detailed the events leading to Japan's war of aggression, explaining that gluttonous profiteering from Japan's capitalists had ensured the nation's imperial expansion and therefore its atrocities in China, Manila, and elsewhere. The film's ending explained that many Japanese war criminals had escaped trial and were still among the population, closing with an evocative crossfade from Hirohito in Imperial regalia to Hirohito in civilian clothing. CIE were naturally involved throughout its production, demanding changes so that certain politicians would remain unnamed as war criminals. Although the film found a limited release, the Occupation eventually seized prints and withdrew the film. Several American officials and Japanese politicians – including the then-prime minister, Shigeru Yoshida – believed the film should be suppressed. Given that the Emperor was central to legitimising the aims of the Occupation, the film's call for Hirohito to face justice was considered incompatible with SCAP's plans (Hirano, 1992, 122–45).

These overtly repressive elements of Occupation control gained momentum in 1947 via the "Reverse Course". The US was increasingly anxious of Soviet activity, as well as the rise of China's Mao Zedong. Japan was therefore to act as a foothold in East Asia against the perceived threat of communist expansion. As such, sweeping anti-trust rulings set to break up the *zeibatsu* (large corporate conglomerates that had profiteered from the war) – as part of the "decentralisation" aspect of SCAP reform – were slowed and then abandoned (Bailey, 1996, 59; Harding, 2019, 258–60). SCAP also intervened over domestic matters significantly. In early 1948, a new wave of dispute actions led by government workers resulted in MacArthur calling for revision of the National Public Service Law, stripping public-sector workers of their right to strike and of their right to collective bargaining (Sims, 2001, 259; Kapur, 2018, 9).

Beginning in 1949, a "red purge" commenced. Some 10,000 communists and socialists were removed from public office, the situation exacerbated by American aggression in Korea and the inflammation of anti-communist suppression. After the *Kyosanto* (Japan Communist Party) adopted more militant tactics, SCAP also purged the 24 members of its Central Committee (Kapur, 2018, 218; Sims, 2001, 263). US imperialism in Korea also aided Japan's economic recovery, with Prime Minister Yoshida calling it a "gift from the gods". US forces under MacArthur's leadership took off from bases on Japanese soil, while UN procurement orders to Japan for materials totalled $240 million by March 1951. In turn, Occupation authorities arrested many Japanese and Korean activists who had worked to disrupt weapon supply lines or disperse anti-war leaflets, handing down sentences of hard labour which were, in many cases, longer than those given to Japan's war criminals (Choi, 2017, 548–51; Okita, 1951, 141–42).

Another development in the Reverse Course was a shift in US priorities toward rearmament. In 1948, US planners called for the expansion of a National Police Reserve, which was officially established in 1950 to be commanded by former Imperial army officers. This Police Reserve played its part in the red purge, with its forces concentrated in areas of *Kyosanto* support (Bailey, 1996, 61–62). The Police Reserve would eventually become Japan's Self Defence Force (JSDF) in 1954.

The "End" of the Occupation

The official end of the Occupation began with the signing of the Peace Treaty in San Francisco on 8 September 1951, which came into effect the following April. On the same day, the US–Japan Security Treaty was also signed. Of its terms, one of the most dangerous was the allowance of a large American military presence in Japan. It also permitted US troops to intervene over domestic crises if requested by the Japanese government. There was, however, no specific commitment for the US to defend Japan (Packard, 1966, 6–7). In the realm of domestic politics, Japan's Left condemned the treaty for aligning Japan with American Cold War policy; the Right criticised it on nationalist grounds (Bailey, 1996, 64). Such responses were a precursor to the political movements that opposition to both the US and the Treaty would inspire as the 1950s wore on.

Post-War Japan and *Godzilla*

The nature of the US Occupation had been enormous in scale and implementation, matched only by the swiftness with which some reforms were altered or abandoned, and by the many continuities that connected pre-war and post-war systems of power. Fervent anti-communism had shaped US reform policy, partly facilitating the eventual return of several wartime Japanese leaders to political life. It was within this context that Toho's *Godzilla* appeared in November 1954.

Ghidorah, the Three-Headed Monster

Earlier that year, the spectre of nuclear warfare resurfaced in an event which the US Defence Nuclear Agency would eventually call "the worst single incident of fallout exposures in all the US atmospheric testing program" (Weisgall, 1994, 304).

In July 1946, less than a year after the atomic bombings of Hiroshima and Nagasaki, the United States embarked on Operation Crossroads, the first of many nuclear test series in the Pacific. As the devices became more intricate and their yields more monstrous in scale, hydrogen weapons soon entered the equation. On 1 March 1954, the US would detonate the largest thermonuclear weapon in its history. The device, *Bravo*, was a hydrogen weapon exploded as part of the Castle series of tests. Though its predicted yield was six megatons (equivalent to six million tons of TNT), it ended up closer to 15, equal to the force of about 750 Hiroshima bombs. Exploded at Bikini Atoll in the Marshall Islands, *Bravo* violently contributed to the ongoing displacement of Bikini's people and greatly irradiated its ecology. *Bravo*'s fallout was also scattered over the 236 inhabitants of Rongelap and Utrik atolls about 100 miles away (Weisgall, 1994, 302–03).

The fallout from *Bravo* also reached a Japanese fishing boat, the *Lucky Dragon No.5*. The crewmembers and their catch of tuna were heavily irradiated, and radio operator Akichi Kuboyama eventually succumbed to radiation sickness. The opening of *Godzilla* sees the crew of a similar fishing boat witnessing a bright flash of light before their ship is incinerated. The parallel is striking. This is our entry to explore what *Godzilla* means, as well as how the themes and ideas of subsequent Godzilla films align or differ.

The original scenario for the film by novelist Shigeru Kayama was even more forthright in its connection to the *Lucky Dragon* disaster, directly referencing the event as well as wider American nuclear tests in the Pacific (Angles in Kayama, 2023, 197–200). When director Ishiro Honda was assigned to *Godzilla*, he and co-writer Takeo Murata ultimately toned down Kayama's more direct commentary in their adapted screenplay – instead pursuing broader, global concerns about nuclear weapons – but these events nevertheless remain integral to the presentation of *Godzilla*'s imagery. Japanese audiences were still very much aware of what *Godzilla*'s opening stood for.

Honda would similarly remain open about Godzilla's symbolism: "we wanted [the monster] to possess the terrifying characteristics of an atomic bomb. This was our approach, without any reservations" (Ryfle & Godziszewski, 2017, 84–85).

Following the *Lucky Dragon* parallel that opens *Godzilla*, the same fate befalls other ships. The culprit also ravages nearby Odo Island, emerging from the sea cloaked in – or perhaps an extension of – a massive storm. A scientific party investigates. Among the group are Dr. Yamane (Takashi Shimura), his daughter, Emiko (Momoko Kochi), and her lover, Ogata (Akira Takarada). The expedition finds prehistoric trilobites and radioactive material in the beast's footprints, pointing to its ancient origin and modern threat. The monster comes ashore, and our characters have their first proper look at Godzilla.

Yamane theorises that H-bomb testing has awakened the beast. Fascinated by its ability to survive, he hauntingly remarks, "Godzilla was baptised in the fire of the hydrogen bomb. How can we kill it?"

Godzilla twice lays waste to Tokyo. After witnessing hospitals filled with irradiated survivors, Emiko tells Ogata about a secret invention by an enigmatic scientist and war veteran named Dr. Serizawa (Akihiko Hirata). Serizawa and Emiko were expected to be married, but before she could tell him about Ogata, she witnessed his creation: the Oxygen Destroyer. Serizawa's chemical compound destroys all nearby oxygen when activated, reducing organic life to bone. Ogata and Emiko plead with Serizawa to use the weapon against Godzilla. He initially refuses, fearful that it may fall into the wrong hands. After hearing a news broadcast of a prayer for peace, Serizawa relents.

Gathered in Tokyo Bay, Yamane, Emiko, and dozens of onlookers watch as Ogata and Serizawa are lowered into the sea. Once they near Godzilla, Ogata heads to the surface. Serizawa does not follow; he activates the Oxygen Destroyer and cuts his line. As the device begins to work, he wishes Emiko and Ogata happiness. Godzilla disintegrates as the ocean boils.

With Serizawa and Godzilla destroyed, Yamane offers a few chilling words: "If nuclear testing continues, then someday, somewhere in the world, another Godzilla may appear". The film ends as it began: looking out at the sea.

Ghidorah, the Three-Headed Monster

In the late 1950s, Japanese film critics debated whether the science-fiction film was separate from or the next evolution of the *kaiki eiga* (the "strange" or "bizarre" film, generally referring to a thread of atmospheric, gothic, and/or period-set pictures typified by Nobuo Nakagawa's ghost stories and eventually Britain's Hammer horror films). As the then-emergent *kaiju eiga* (the "strange beast" film, of which *Godzilla* remains the essential urtext) is generally understood as science fiction, it too is separate from the *kaiki eiga* (Crandol in Fujiki & Phillips, 2020, 298–308; Crandol, 2019, 20–22). However, while the *kaiki eiga* should not be considered interchangeable as a term with the more generic "horror", examining *Godzilla* through a horror lens helps to clarify some of its more personal dimensions. In particular, the genre descriptions provided by Vivian Sobchack can structure examination.

Of course, Sobchack's writing refers primarily to American films of the mid-twentieth century, but *Godzilla*'s inception was influenced by and in conversation with American cinema. Eiji Tsuburaya was, for example, a devotee of the original *King Kong* (1933, Merian C. Cooper & Ernest B. Schoedsack), the imagery of which remains foundational to the giant monster film (Ryfle & Godziszewski, 2017, 86–88). In 1952, RKO re-released *Kong* to massive success, leading to an independent monster film about a dinosaur awakened by an atomic test in the Arctic circle: *The Beast from 20,000 Fathoms* (1953, Eugene Lourie). Although *The Beast* was released in Japan shortly after *Godzilla*, producer Tomoyuki Tanaka (aware of trends and international film news) was likely already conscious of the film and its considerable financial success – evidenced by an early proposal for *Godzilla* titled *The Giant Monster from 20,000 Miles Under the Sea*. In turn, later Western giant monster entries like the King Brothers' *Gorgo* (1961, Eugene Lourie) and the Danish–American *Reptilicus* (1961, Sidney Pink & Poul Bang) drew from Toho's monster films (Pink, 1989, 90). Concurrently, this is not to suggest that Japanese and American monster films of the era were or are identical, either – narratively, thematically, or aesthetically. When reviewing *Godzilla*, for example, the *Mainichi Shimbun* contrasted the film's handling of its central metaphor with that of *The Beast*, noting the more focused, specific expression of atomic fears in Honda's film (Ryfle & Godziszewski, 2017, 104–05). Rather, while acknowledging national specificities, consideration of transnational cross-pollination (Rawle, 2022, 15–20) means that although Sobchack's genre descriptions cannot be completely all-encompassing, they can still provide a framework with which to structure analysis.

Sobchack's writing on the lone individual in the horror film is pertinent, a character in conflict with society or some extension of himself; a character who transgresses laws (spiritual or societal) and who suffers and dies as a consequence. While both science fiction and horror, according to Sobchack, concern chaos and disruption, the former is broad and societal in scope, while the latter is personalised and moral in nature (Sobchack, 2004, 29–52).

Michael Crandol (2019, 21) situates *Godzilla* away from the *kaiki eiga* (and horror more generally) partly due to what he argues is the film's lack of personalised dread and suspense. Initially, *Godzilla* may appear to align with how Sobchack describes science fiction, when society and its institutions are in conflict with themselves or some alien other, and when the chaos engendered is civil, rather than moral. Godzilla's threat is on an enormous, societal scale by virtue of the monster's literal size and its nuclear origins (with overt suggestions of future reappearances threatening the whole world); its destruction is often seen from a distance by its lead characters; protagonists like Dr. Yamane are scientists working in tandem with the government; and other societal institutions like the military are similarly called upon.

However, Godzilla's chaos is *both* civil and moral, societal and personal. At multiple junctures the film takes time to focus on individual people at Godzilla's mercy, from a frightened mother huddled with her children in the flames of Tokyo, to another child being scanned with a Geiger counter by a despairing doctor in the aftermath. More specifically, the historical tensions engendered by Godzilla's origins are personally reflected in the moral turmoil of Dr. Serizawa. He is the lone figure in conflict with both society *and* an extension of himself, a framework which fits his ties to wartime Japan, his complicated, stilted relationships with others like Emiko, his guilt over having created a dreadful superweapon, his moral dilemma in using the weapon against Godzilla, and in his ultimate self-sacrifice to ensure that it is never used again. Serizawa does not reckon with Godzilla as if he were its direct creator; but because he has created a weapon which he himself compares to atomic and hydrogen bombs, he reckons with what the monster represents – what its appearance is a testament to – and for which he feels tremendous guilt for having contributed.

As David Kalat (2010, 21) notes, Serizawa performs a narrative role similar to Godzilla. Both are relics of the past, and Godzilla becomes the extension of Serizawa.

Serizawa is of the past in several ways. He is somewhat akin to Yasujirō Ozu's melancholic parental figures in his later works like *Late Autumn* (1960) and *An Autumn Afternoon* (1962), who seem increasingly aware of how archaic they and their customs have become in post-war Japan. Serizawa's implied arranged engagement to Emiko is made distinct compared to the romance between her and Ogata, emphasised by a filmmaking landscape that had seen CIE censors take issue with perceived feudalistic gender relations, stressing individualism in depictions of relationships (Hirano, 1992, 70–71). Additionally, when Serizawa is asked by a journalist about some German colleagues of his, he fervently denies any links. His anguished insistence suggests potentially sordid wartime activities. Furthermore, Serizawa seldom leaves his laboratory – a shadowy cave of scientific devices accessed at the bottom of a staircase – as though incompatible with the outside world.

Godzilla, the monster, is obviously of the past as a prehistoric creature alive in the present day. More pressingly, however, Godzilla was revived by nuclear weapons, American products of the Second World War. Godzilla immediately haunts Japan as the Bomb made flesh, but also as a memory of the war in which those weapons were created and used. And with their links to the war, both Godzilla and Serizawa are ghosts of Japan's recent past.

Through the processes of surrender and occupation to (superficially) repress Japan's former wartime profile, the imperial project is returned in the body of the monster to terrorise a Westernised, post-war nation. In Inuhiko Yomota's analysis, Godzilla's origins in the Pacific are pertinent to this interpretation. Yomota cites folklorist Kunio Yanagita's theory that the Japanese must meet death in their homeland for their souls to rest peacefully, implying that those who died in the Pacific during the Second World War exist in a state of limbo. Godzilla emerges from the sea as the living embodiment of those unquiet spirits and the past to which they belong (Yomota in Philips & Stringer, 2007, 107–08). Standing in a post-war Tokyo, Godzilla embodies something violent, ugly, and blood-soaked: the processes of change from the war to the present. And in turn, the monster is infinitely multifaceted, evading singular interpretation. The monster is both the Bomb and its victim; it is Japan's wartime aggression resurrected and personified; it is a threat that is personally embodied and of global concern; it is equal parts belligerent and victimised, monstrous and sympathetic.

In an interview conducted for a 2011 DVD release of *Godzilla*, film critic Tadao Sato similarly articulated the monster's layered embodiment of the war in terms of audience identification:

> Oddly enough, the fact you felt more sympathy for the monsters in [Ishiro Honda's monster films] was a pleasant surprise, something that I think kept audiences coming back for a long time. I wonder if that isn't a reflection of the fact Japan lost the war. For a time, we were the monster. When that monster gets cornered by human beings, it's not surprising that it meets its downfall. People watched that quite sympathetically.

At the film's end, Godzilla and Serizawa perish together as symbolic of Japan's recent history, the individual facing the extension of himself. Just as Godzilla, a prehistoric creature, is out of place in the twentieth century, Serizawa is also incapable of adapting because of his irreconcilable ties to the past. If, in part, Godzilla embodies the war, then Godzilla must be destroyed for the post-war order to triumph. All the bloodshed and violence, both Japanese and American, that are mirrored in the monster's form, sound, and aggression, are disintegrated in Tokyo Bay as if to allow the post-war narrative to take hold – a disintegration imposed and reified in reality by the 1947 constitution, the US–Japan Security Treaty, and the rehabilitation of Japan's war criminals.

Moreover, returning to Yomota's identification of Godzilla's Pacific origins to connect the monster with the war dead, it is telling that Serizawa's final resting place returns him to that same site, as if confirming his ties to the wartime past with grave finality. Serizawa's sacrifice and Godzilla's death suggest the closing of a historical chapter and the beginning of another, one that is both reflective of the past (as Sato suggests) and fearful of what the future holds. Thus, as a response to Japan's recent past and its

Ghidorah, the Three-Headed Monster

present anxieties, *Godzilla* sits as part of a wider Japanese film canon that addresses the war, the Bomb, and their legacies in the changing post-war years.

A direct contemporary in this regard is Hideo Sekigawa's *Hiroshima* (1953), which features music by composer Akira Ifukube. While some of the film's major melodies were revised cues originally written in 1947 for Senkichi Taniguchi's *Snow Trail*, their realisation for *Hiroshima* is utterly singular. These reworked cues were used again almost verbatim in *Godzilla*, most notably following the monster's second Tokyo rampage. The music that accompanies a depiction of the atomic bombing of Hiroshima also carries Godzilla's fictional nuclear violence. Thus, from its director's authorial stamp to the very selection of its music, *Godzilla* plays as a tapestry of collective memory and anxiety.

Godzilla was successful for Toho and a sequel soon went into production. *Godzilla Raids Again* (1955, Motoyoshi Oda) arrived six months after its predecessor, lending different but no less urgent post-war perspectives. After Godzilla and new monster Anguirus are discovered brawling on an island, they soon make their way to Osaka and lay waste to the city. Framing their conflict is a cast led by Hiroshi Koizumi, a fresh-faced rising star for Toho who would go on to perform in several genre pictures – including *Ghidorah, the Three-Headed Monster*. The film depicts Godzilla and Anguirus interrupting the lives of Tsukioka (Koizumi), a pilot for a fishing company, and those in his circle. As such, the film offers a compelling slice-of-life quality. These are not top scientists, journalists, or military personnel. They are not even adjacent to the roles usually associated with contemporary monster-film narratives. This provides a from-the-ground perspective of lives disrupted and even cut short by the monsters.

Godzilla's symbolism as a wartime phantom is resurrected to terrorise domesticity. *Godzilla Raids Again* thrusts horror and violence over people who lack even the narrative qualifications to fight back. These are civilians caught in the action. Godzilla and Anguirus suggest both wartime and post-war experience in this respect. When Godzilla approaches Osaka, a citywide blackout is instituted, reminiscent of such practices during the war to ward off Allied bombing. We also witness Japanese fighter planes heading out to sea over the eerily darkened city with similar connotations. Godzilla once again appears as an embodiment of wartime memory returned to stalk the post-war arena. Meanwhile, the film's characters, trapped by the incredible forces of these enormous creatures, also recall a Japanese population coming to terms with similarly massive constitutional, social, and political change imposed from above via the US Occupation.

Furthermore, in a scene following Godzilla and Anguirus' Osaka rampage, the characters look out over the decimated city. Despite the utter devastation which surrounds them, their homes and haunts obliterated, they speak of picking up their tools to start over. The narratives of post-war rebirth resurface.

Politically, 1955 would also see Japan's various conservative forces consolidated into the Liberal Democratic Party (LDP) in November (Sims, 2001, 274–75). This unification was significant, for the LDP have ruled almost uninterrupted ever since. Nevertheless, the LDP's fortunes would fluctuate, with the actions of its leaders proving both wildly unpopular and historically significant in the years to come – the effects of which would be felt in Toho's monster pictures.

As the 1950s wore on, Toho's special effects output became more spectacular with the introduction of colour photography. The year 1956 saw the release of *Rodan* (Ishiro Honda), which also addresses nuclear concerns but in a broader manner. *Rodan* sees a pair of giant Pteranodon-like creatures emerge from the bowels of the Earth. It is theorised that nuclear testing may have awakened them – a connection made explicit in a newly created prologue for the King Brothers' US release. In turn, *Rodan* subtly evokes the evolving and difficult US–Japan relationship in the appearance and demise of its monsters. Its ending sees a barrage of rockets launched at Mount Aso to engulf the Rodans in an eruption. The weapons used are "Honest John" missiles of American manufacture, a fact emphasised in publicity and reviews for the film's US release. Thus, while the Rodans' appearance implicates US culpability via nuclear testing, it is also US weaponry that provides the film's resolution – recalling America's contradictory position in Japan's post-war narrative.

While *Rodan* was one of Toho's first colour special effects films, *The Mysterians* (1957, Ishiro Honda) blasted audiences with widescreen Tohoscope. More pressingly than *Rodan*, *The Mysterians* embodies the US–Japan relationship. In the film, the Mysterians are a dying race, victims of a massive atomic war which consumed their society. They occupy Japanese land and desire human women with whom they can breed to preserve their species, promising destruction via giant robots and flying saucers if their terms are not met. The image of an invading force, occupying Japanese land with terrifyingly powerful technology and exploiting its women, naturally calls the US Occupation to mind. Fears of what Allied troops would do upon arrival at the war's end were widespread, and sexual violence committed by US servicemen was reported within weeks of their arrival (Tanaka, 2002, 112–17). However, this does not provide a complete historical situation of the film, for Japan itself enforced gendered violence as an occupying force both before and during the Second World War. Japan's so-called "comfort stations" in conquered territories saw as many as 100,000 to 250,000 women forced into sexual slavery – tens of thousands of whom would die before they could be freed (McClain, 2001, 497).

That the Mysterians kidnap multiple women to commodify their bodies, making them tools in the course of their conquest, recalls similar Imperial Japanese violence. It also calls to mind director Ishiro Honda's wartime experience. Honda was drafted in 1935 at the age of 23 and was called to the front three times before the war's end. Between 1940 and 1941, he was assigned to monitor one of Japan's comfort stations. Honda addressed this part of his life in an essay published in 1966, explaining that he would listen to the personal stories and testimonies of the women enslaved at the station as part of his job, recalling horrific treatment and lives destroyed (Ryfle & Godziszewski, 2017, 15–33). Without trivialising or flattening the details of Honda's involvement in Japan's wartime atrocities, the reflections of Imperial Japan in the Mysterians intersect with both national and individual action.

The war shaped Honda's outlook and informed his wish to see international co-operation – "the coming together of all humankind as one to create a peaceful society" (Ryfle & Godziszewski, 2017, 137) – and this is at the forefront of *The Mysterians*. The image of East and West, united against the Mysterian threat, seems broadly optimistic given both recent memories of war and contemporary politics. The year 1957 saw the launch of the Soviet satellite, *Sputnik-1*, which caused consternation in Japan over how closely it should align with US policy given the new reality of Inter-Continental Ballistic Missiles. That year also saw the LDP's Nobusuke Kishi become Japanese prime minister.

Kishi had firm connections to Imperial Japan, having served as an official in Manchukuo between 1936 and 1939. Kishi openly espoused racism against the Chinese, believing them to be nothing more than obedient tools at his disposal for the Taylorist labour policies he had marvelled at in Europe and America in the 1920s. Mark Driscoll (2010, 270) has written that "when Kishi merged the Euro-American codes of labour management and economic planning with the ingrained habitus of Japanese colonial rule... the result was an almost seamless system well lubed to join the means of industrial capitalism with the ends of total war and death". Kishi would enact further policies of forced and slave labour, with millions more worked to death after Japan launched its full-scale invasion of China and prisoners of war were sent to Manchukuo (Driscoll, 2010, 266–77). Returning to Japan, Kishi served as vice minister of commerce and minister of munitions in Hideki Tojo's wartime cabinet. As part of that cabinet, he had been a co-signer of Japan's declaration of war and was eventually imprisoned as a suspected war criminal but was released after three years in Sugamo Prison (Packard, 1966, 49; Bailey, 1996, 82). In the post-war years, Kishi was an avid supporter of rearmament, close ties with the US, and constitutional revision. He would make revision of the US–Japan Security Treaty a primary goal of his tenure, galvanising firm opposition to him, the Treaty, and the US in the following years.

In 1958, Honda was assigned to another rumination on the dangers of nuclear weapons: *The H-Man*. The film's opening evokes the *Lucky Dragon* disaster even more so than that of *Godzilla*: we see an atomic explosion before a newspaper headline tells of a missing boat at sea. The film is about mutant, liquid sailors who have returned to Japan after high exposure to radioactive fallout. The film blends horror and crime drama as the H-Men interrupt a police investigation into drug smuggling.

The film's basic premise, that nuclear testing has mutated people into liquid creatures, prompts further consideration. In the titular H-Men, the film is concerned with the Bomb's effect on the body, how radiation affects people, and what happens when these people return home. In turn, the film draws the *hibakusha* experience to mind. Japan's *hibakusha* ("atomic-bomb-affected person"), the survivors of Hiroshima and Nagasaki, have faced significant social ostracism on top of lingering health effects.

Many have chosen to hide their experience altogether, lest they face further exclusion and difficulty when seeking employment. Fumio Kamei's 1956 documentary film, *It's Good to Live*, presents the *hibakusha* experience with candour, conveying lives forever changed by the atomic bombings, and often describing terrible alienation. Hideo Sekigawa's *Hiroshima* similarly depicts *hibakusha* isolation in the post-war years.

In 1946, the US established the Atomic Bomb Casualty Commission (ABCC) to survey atomic bomb survivors and their health. The screening process was utterly demeaning, with people's bodies examined and photographed; young women felt particularly vulnerable, with girls seen nude in some cases. Moreover, no medical care was given to ease the ailments many *hibakusha* faced (Southard, 2016, 178–84).

The treatment of the *hibakusha*, from the cold degradation of the ABCC screenings to the public isolation they were made to feel, is othering writ large. Their experience was treated as a scientific curiosity on one hand and as a source of public disconnection on the other. While at face value the liquid people of *The H-Man* may appear frightening or monstrous, they possess an urgent poignancy – especially when one scientist explains that they may have retained the minds of the people they once were. They are victims of nuclear proliferation, human beings so irrevocably changed that they cannot properly return home, and viewed with horror by those around them. Through the film's invocation of the Bomb's bodily harm and the disconnection it engenders, *The H-Man* runs parallel to the *hibakusha* experience, illustrating how Toho's genre films were directly and indirectly contributing to culture-wide expressions of Japan's relationship to the Bomb, memories of mass devastation, and society's transformation.

Godzilla, meanwhile, had been in a state of partial hibernation since 1955 – partial in that the monster would not reappear in a film until 1962. However, Godzilla would appear in other mediums, most notably manga. It is through these comic appearances that Godzilla's personality and image shifted before these elements similarly changed in the films. Several adaptations of both *Godzilla* and *Godzilla Raids Again* appeared in manga form, many of which depicted Godzilla in comic fashion and took significant plot liberties. One adaptation of *Godzilla* by Shigeru Sugiura sees a child deliver the Oxygen Destroyer to Godzilla, notably dropping the self-sacrificial element (Gerow in Tsutsui & Ito, 2006, 68). This also illustrates how children were part of Godzilla's audience from the very beginning, long before they became its key focus by the end of the following decade. These adaptations similarly foreshadowed the softening of the series' post-war anxieties in the 1960s and beyond (Igarashi, 2000, 121). Moreover, Shigeru Mizuki's 1958 manga, *Kaiju Raban*, took Godzilla into wild science-fiction territory long before the films did, depicting a monster created from Godzilla's cells – which eventually became a narrative staple of the series in the late 1980s and 1990s.

Meanwhile, a recurring group of production staff members had been consolidated for Toho's monster films: producer Tomoyuki Tanaka, director Ishiro Honda, special effects director Eiji Tsuburaya, composer Akira Ifukube, and screenwriters Takeshi Kimura (a.k.a. Kaoru Mabuchi) and Shinichi Sekizawa. In particular, Sekizawa would be instrumental in steering the tonal shifts and narrative styles that emerged in the 1960s, indelibly influencing the rest of the Godzilla series.

Into the 1960s

The year 1960 witnessed some of the largest protests in Japan's political history, firmly against renewal of the US–Japan Security Treaty. Tensions and anti-American sentiment had grown throughout the 1950s in response to US military violence and expansion, contributing to the momentum which exploded at the onset of the new decade.

As established, one of the Security Treaty's most dangerous terms was the allowance of a large US military presence on Japanese soil. Throughout the 1950s, anti-American sentiment grew alongside early political attempts at revision of the Treaty, such as Foreign Minister Mamoru Shigemitsu leading a delegation to the US in 1955 – only to be rebuffed by Secretary of State John Foster Dulles (Sims, 2001, 281). Meanwhile, major struggles were initiated all over Japan against expansion of US artillery ranges and air bases. For example, between 1955 and 1957, locals in Sunagawa protested the expansion of runways at the nearby Tachikawa Air Base.

Also in 1957, the violence of continued American military presence in Japan was exemplified by a US serviceman named William S. Girard, who murdered a mother of six named Naka Sakai on a US-leased firing range. The case caused international dispute over how Girard would be tried. His commander initially refused to transfer him to Japanese jurisdiction, prompting massive outcry. The Eisenhower administration eventually relented, and Girard was tried in Japanese court. He received just a three-year suspended sentence (Packard, 1966, 35–36; Kapur, 2018, 17).

When it came time to renew the US–Japan Security Treaty at the end of the decade, Nobusuke Kishi had negotiated the removal of some of its terms. The US would no longer be allowed to put down internal disturbances if requested; the US would be obliged to defend Japan in case of attack; and the US had to consult Japan before any major changes in the deployment of personnel on Japanese soil. Additionally, the new Treaty had a ten-year term, after which it could be repealed by either side with one year's notice (Kapur, 2018, 17–18; Bailey, 1996, 85–86).

Kishi had hoped these changes would be broadly popular, but his unscrupulous use of Diet procedure preceded his undoing. In 1958, as he was renegotiating the Security Treaty, Kishi had rushed a controversial bill through the Diet revising the Police Duties Law, expanding police powers of warrantless search and seizure. Then, in 1960, Kishi similarly rushed the revised Treaty itself through the Diet so that its ratification preceded a visit by President Eisenhower. As Nick Kapur (2018, 23) explains,

> This was a crafty maneuver because under Diet rules at the time, any treaty passed by the lower house would automatically be approved after thirty days, even without action by the upper house, as long as the Diet remained in session during that time. By passing the treaty through the lower house on May 20, Kishi ensured that the treaty would be automatically ratified at midnight on June 19, just in time for Eisenhower's arrival in Japan later that day.

Protests erupted, the largest of which took place on 15 June 1960. A nationwide strike of 6.4 million workers was held, with a massive demonstration in front of the Diet building. Student protestors managed to storm their way in, but police violence was extreme; a Tokyo University undergraduate named Michiko Kanba was killed. Kishi was ultimately successful in getting his Treaty revisions ratified, but the significant opposition protests – helped in part by television coverage stirring public support – forced him to resign.

Commentary on the US–Japan Security Treaty is evident in 1961's *Mothra*. Originally existing in serialised form as *The Luminous Fairies and Mothra*, screenwriter Shinichi Sekizawa adapted it for the screen. *Mothra* tells the story of the titular creature wreaking havoc across Japan to save two tiny women (the Shobijin) who are kidnapped from Mothra's home on Infant Island by shady entrepreneur Clark Nelson (Jerry Ito). Direct commentary on the Security Treaty appeared in its serialised form, and the final film still carries these politics in its depiction of the fictional nation of Rolisica (as a stand-in for the US) and the consequences of greed. The film and its politics will be discussed in Chapter Three, but pertinent to this discussion is how *Mothra* carries its politics in a light-hearted manner.

The scripts of Shinichi Sekizawa are seldom considered very political, especially when compared with the more sombre work of his counterpart, Takeshi Kimura (a.k.a. Kaoru Mabuchi). This belief has been furthered by Ishiro Honda, who, in a 1992 interview with David Milner, said that "Sekizawa had a more humanistic touch and a very joyous – at times humorous – sensibility", adding that, "he was not the type to write about social issues" (Honda in Mirjahangir, 2022). Sekizawa himself echoed that assessment when, speaking about *Mothra*, he said, "It's fundamentally upbeat. It was a great fit for my personality, since I'm also an upbeat person, so to speak" (Sekizawa in Endo, 1985a, 162).

Despite these testimonies, Sekizawa's body of science-fiction work still offers social relevance, seen especially in *Atragon* (1963, Ishiro Honda). The film concerns the ancient undersea Mu Empire rising to conquer the surface world. Jun Tazaki plays Captain Jinguji, a former Imperial naval officer who has lived on an island since the end of the Second World War, refusing to accept defeat – evoking myriad real-life cases of Japanese soldiers who survived for years in isolation on islands after the war. Jinguji has built the Gotengo, a massive warship with which he plans to restore the Japanese Empire. His former commanding officer, Admiral Kusumi (Ken Uehara), locates him and asks that he use the Gotengo against Mu, but Jinguji refuses.

Sekizawa and Honda depict past meeting present, Jinguji's jingoism nullified by the passage of time and the new face of Japan represented by the younger cast members – especially Jinguji's daughter (Yoko Fujiyama). The Empress of Mu, with her war-crazed fanaticism, is Jinguji's reflection; he eventually relents and uses the Gotengo to save the world. For all its visual spectacle, *Atragon* shows Sekizawa's capability with more mature themes, openly criticising the futility of nationalism while suggesting the possibility of change.

Moreover, Sekizawa was aware of world trends and would embed them into his scripts. In a 1985 interview, Sekizawa was asked if he incorporated topical events into his work, to which he responded, "Yes, I do. I don't know if 'incorporate' is the right word. I don't analyse it too much. Whatever is big news at the time is something I add in. Whatever is going on in the zeitgeist makes its way into the script" (Sekizawa in Endo, 1985b, 196).

Nevertheless, the predominant characteristic of Sekizawa's work is an upbeat manner. As Honda said, "if the story were very positive or even childlike, it would go to Sekizawa" (Ryfle & Godziszewski, 2017, 172). While Sekizawa stated that his approach was to focus on producing entertaining images and not to stress fine details (Sekizawa in Endo, 1985a, 160–61), the positive outlook many of his scripts espouse is worth examining given the contexts of Japan at the time. For example, what does the fairytale happy ending of *Mothra* mean when considering the real-life narratives of the Security Treaty that had informed its inception?

Sekizawa acknowledged the tonal shifts between *Mothra* and prior films when (in a comparison tense with regional histories and perceptions thereof) he observed that,

> If you look at Rodan or any of its ilk, they fundamentally come from a darker place, right? There's something moody about them. But Mothra was the first monster that was styled as coming from a Polynesian place. Take *Giant Monster Varan* [1958, Ishiro Honda], or movies set in some remote part of northeastern Japan, or Mount Aso: these monsters always come from some deep and dark place. But Mothra was the first from a remote island, something never seen before, it wasn't a scary character in the way the others were. It was sort of... fantastic, or should I say, the colouring and styling, the expression. Mothra could never come from a dark and gloomy place. (Sekizawa in Endo, 1985a, 161–62)

Sekizawa's scriptwriting ethos would steer the Godzilla series in the 1960s, retaining social relevance but nonetheless easing the anxiety of prior films via lighter entertainment – mirroring a Japan moving further from the memories of war.

Godzilla Returns to the Screen

The mass television coverage of the Security Treaty protests was a sign of the times: TV ownership had dramatically increased in the 1950s. While television sets were extraordinarily expensive when broadcasts began in the early 1950s, costs fell as the economy recovered. For example, a domestic set cost about ¥175,000 ($500) in 1953, but by 1958 the price had fallen to ¥60,000 ($167). In line with price drops and rising incomes, television ownership in Tokyo households grew from around 10% in 1957 to 42.3% in 1960, with similar increases across other Japanese cities (Chun, 2007, 72). Indeed, sales of television sets increased from 1.5 million in 1958 to 3.5 million in 1959 (Kitaura in Fujiki & Phillips, 2020, 119).

The early 1950s saw a rivalry between public and private broadcasters (NHK and NTV, respectively). It was argued that NTV would concentrate on urban viewers to the exclusion of those in the countryside, while NHK was accused of shutting out all but the very wealthy with its exorbitant subscription costs for public broadcasting. Within this conflict, NHK aimed to pursue "high-brow" entertainment centred on art, politics, and news. Meanwhile, NTV focused on mass entertainment to court greater numbers for maximum profitability. As televisions were still too expensive to buy for most, sets in communal areas drew massive crowds. Within this arena, pro-wrestling proved a lucrative broadcast choice for NTV (Chun, 2007, 54–62).

Rikidōzan was Japan's star wrestler, tapping into a post-war nationalism as he clobbered foreign opponents to audience cries of "Nippon banzai!" ("Long Live Japan"). Rikidōzan's cultural footprint extended beyond the ring, starring in dozens of films as himself. Such was his popularity that Rikidōzan and Masahiko Kimura's three-day match with the Sharpe Brothers in 1954 was viewed by 900,000 people (Chun, 2007, 63).

Ghidorah, the Three-Headed Monster

This background set the stage for Godzilla's first appearance in seven years, the colour Tohoscope spectacle of *King Kong vs. Godzilla* (1962, Ishiro Honda). Kong and Godzilla's battle is framed with deliberate satiric wit from Sekizawa, presenting an absurd exaggeration of TV's pro-wrestling fixation. Japanese comedy legend Ichiro Arishima plays Mr. Tako, publicity manager for Pacific Pharmaceuticals, who believes the company needs a new representative to drive up ratings for the programmes they sponsor. Naturally, Tako turns to the biggest representative around: King Kong. While Tako brings Kong to Japan from his home on Faro Island, a United Nations submarine accidentally frees Godzilla from its iceberg tomb. When Tako is prevented from bringing Kong into the country, the giant ape makes his own way there – just as Godzilla continues its march the same way. The film's climax sees the pair battle at the base of Mount Fuji before tumbling into the sea.

King Kong vs. Godzilla is a defining moment for the Godzilla series in shifting the tone toward lighter entertainment, yet its political and cultural underpinnings remain sharp. The East-versus-West nationalist fervour of Rikidōzan's fights with Western opponents translates to the mythologised battle between Kong and Godzilla. Indeed, Inuhiko Yomota argues that here Godzilla stands in for Japanese nationalism against the American opponent (Yomota, 2019, 118). However, Yoshikuni Igarashi (2000, 121) sees the conflict as a replication of the foundational post-war narrative of America (via Kong) saving Japan from itself (Godzilla), rendering the East-versus-West interpretation more complex. The recreated conflict is further complicated because Rikidōzan was Korean-born; he came to Japan in 1940 as a sumo hopeful. His personal history, and therefore its interaction with Japan's colonial violence in Korea, was obscured in service of a public persona and narrative that provided a Japanese avatar in the reimagined wartime arena (Igarashi, 2000, 123–24). Kong and Godzilla's exaggerated battle similarly flattens the tensions of several historical sites and contexts into an easily consumable wrestling match.

The film also proved that Godzilla could take on genre trappings other than horror and science fiction. Comedy was now in the mix as the film borrows the formula of contemporary Japanese "salaryman" comedies (which satirised the office politics of white-collar workers). This is also exemplified by the film's cast, with actors like Tadao Takashima and Ichiro Arishima appearing in many such films. Moreover, the beginning of Godzilla's personality change was set in motion. Quoted in the film's original 1962 programme booklet, special effects director Eiji Tsuburaya said, "the acting of the monsters was significantly increased in this film. The monsters express feelings, and they have personalities. In this case, we set Godzilla as the bad guy, and King Kong is kind of like a comedian".

Monstrous Economic Revival

The rise in television ownership was partly facilitated by Japan's post-war economic recovery. For example, between 1952 and 1958, Japan's gross domestic product (GDP) grew at an average rate of 7%, which jumped to a staggering 13% between 1959 and 1961 – the highest in the world. Moreover, Japan's exports tripled between 1952 and 1960, and in 1956 Japan surpassed Britain as the world's leading shipbuilder (Packard, 1966, 34).

Following Kishi's resignation, the LDP's Hayato Ikeda became Japanese prime minister. During his tenure, Ikeda boosted Japan's economic revival, phasing out stagnating industries and investing in steel, oil refining, and petrochemicals – adversely affecting Japan's environment in the process. This was accompanied by an increase in consumer goods like electronics, synthetic fibres, and cars. Consequently, Japan's growth rate eventually reached an average of 10% by 1965, compared with 4.8% in the US and 3.4% in Britain (Bailey, 1996, 90).

Mothra vs. Godzilla would satirise such staggering growth by repurposing the themes of *Mothra* to great effect. This will be discussed in Chapter Three, but for the contextual purposes of this first chapter we will point to *Mothra*'s depiction of greed stirring the wrath of a monster. That depiction reappears in *Mothra vs. Godzilla*, which sees Mothra's egg wash up in Japan during a typhoon. The Shobijin appeal for the egg's return, but disaster capitalists Torahata (Kenji Sahara) and Kumayama (Yoshifumi Tajima) have already "purchased" the egg to make an attraction. As with *Mothra*'s malevolent Clark Nelson, *Mothra vs. Godzilla* criticises greed via Torahata and Kumayama, allowing for a reflection on Japan's economic recovery.

Ghidorah, the Three-Headed Monster

At this point in the series, we can observe the monsters' symbolism beginning to expand and diverge, shifting away from dread-filled worries of scientific irresponsibility and memories of war – as in *Godzilla*, *Rodan*, *The Mysterians*, *Giant Monster Varan*, and *The H-Man* – and towards more contemporary facets of 1960s post-war Japan, from satirised pop-cultural fixations in *King Kong vs. Godzilla* to capitalistic greed in *Mothra vs. Godzilla*. With these new avenues of symbolism, the monsters' narrative functions change as well.

This is because the constant reappearance of the monsters across these sequels renders their existence relatively normal, no longer a major source of crisis and unrest. These sequels necessitate and then sustain a transformation of the monsters' characterisation and narrative role. In turn, this set the stage for *Ghidorah, the Three-Headed Monster* to fully realise these tonal, narrative, and character shifts, demonstrating that the monsters themselves could be the source of resolution.

When *Ghidorah, the Three-Headed Monster* arrived in December 1964, it would serve not only as the culmination of series changes, but also as a reflection of Japan's carefully constructed new image. Nearly two decades had passed since the war's end, and the impact of the US Occupation on the country's post-war recovery was still unfolding. *Godzilla* and its genre successors wrestled with, responded to, and evoked these historical processes in a variety of ways, from Godzilla as victim and embodiment of the atomic bomb to Godzilla as personification of the Imperial war machine. The symbolism deliberately attached to the October 1964 Tokyo Olympics (discussed in Chapter Three) presented new images of Japan to the world, and *Ghidorah* would show a new kind of Godzilla.

Chapter Two: The Making of *Ghidorah, the Three-Headed Monster*

The 1950s witnessed the second golden age of Japan's film industry, with an astonishing 547 films produced in 1959 (Galbraith, 1996, 1). At the time, double bills at cinemas were already a standard exhibition practice. Individual theatres had contracts with several studios and would often pair films from different companies. Invariably, the films shown on the lower half of a double bill were less profitable, held in that position by unfavourable power dynamics between studios. For example, Toho had a stifling contract with industry-newcomer Toei (formed in 1951), placing the latter's films on the lower half of double bills. In response, Toei set out to beat the larger studios by mass-producing films and supplying exhibitors with double-feature packages of two instead of one. This was mutually beneficial because it was cheaper for exhibitors to sign a contract with a single studio. Toei's enormous success – gaining exhibition contracts and constructing its own cinemas for direct control – made it an industry heavyweight in just a few years. The major studios (including Toho, Daiei, Shochiku, and Nikkatsu) reacted by increasing the scale and number of their own productions – though not without difficulty or consternation (Kitaura in Fujiki & Phillips, 2020, 117–18; Sharp, 2011, 251–52; Anderson & Richie, 1982, 239–40).

Ultimately, this movement was unsustainable and would contribute to an industry-wide decline by the end of the 1960s, signs of which were already visible as early as 1961. Nevertheless, it was within this industry environment that *Ghidorah, the Three-Headed Monster* was produced.

As Nobutaka Suzuki's research shows, producer Tomoyuki Tanaka was interviewed by Jiji Press on 11 April 1964. In the interview, Tanaka mentioned that he was interested in creating a story that would feature Godzilla, Mothra, and King Kong meeting at Mount Fuji. A few days later, on 14 April, the Tokyo *Chunichi Shimbun* reported that an "all-star" monster cast had been planned for an end-of-year movie involving Godzilla, Mothra, and Rodan. And by early August, Toho's monthly nationwide meeting of its branch presidents planned for this film – which would eventually become *Ghidorah* – to be made post-October 1964 (Suzuki in Kimura, 2023, 81–82).

On 19 August, before the film's first script draft had been finalised, the Tokyo edition of *Nikkan Sports* reported on the film's overall story. It also featured a quote from Tanaka, who explained their approach to the new picture:

> Toho's special effects unit has created a dozen-plus monsters to date, but our recent fare has been focused on pitting existing monsters against each other, such as with *King Kong vs. Godzilla* and *Mothra vs. Godzilla*. At a casual glance, [*Ghidorah*] may seem like more of the same, but the reality is quite different. If anything, we always wanted to pit monsters against each other in this fashion, which is why we've created so many different monsters to date. Around three years ago, we began planning this film, which is loosely modelled on a meeting between the US and the USSR. The notion is that the three parties at the table must co-operate to broker world peace. The monsters are anthropomorphised in this film and are each imbued with a personality of sorts. Mr. Tsuburaya, who is directing the special effects, is enthusiastic about using a whole bag of tricks in the special effects team's playbook to make this the pinnacle of monster movies to date. (Tanaka in Kimura, 2023, 82)

Script Drafts and Cast Members

Shinichi Sekizawa was assigned to write the screenplay, turning in his first draft on 27 August 1964. The first draft differs from the finished film in several ways. To contextualise these differences, we must first consider another Toho monster film that Sekizawa also penned in 1964, *Space Monster Dogora* (Ishiro Honda), which was released in Japan a few weeks prior to completion of the first *Ghidorah* draft. *Dogora* concerns a jellyfish-like amoeba that arrives on Earth seeking carbon, clashing with a web of diamond-smuggling gangsters. The film shares several cast members with *Ghidorah*, notably Yosuke Natsuki, Akiko Wakabayashi, and Hiroshi Koizumi.

Yosuke Natsuki had entered the film industry in the late 1950s, debuting in *The H-Man* in a bit part at the request of Tomoyuki Tanaka. On a contract with Toho, he was eventually earning ¥100,000 per month, which he used to buy expensive sports cars (Homenick, 2016). He went on to appear in several high-profile Toho pictures,

Ghidorah, the Three-Headed Monster

from war movies directed by Shue Matsubayashi to Akira Kurosawa's *Yojimbo* (1961). Through these pictures, Natsuki developed a good friendship with Toshiro Mifune, Akira Takarada, Jun Tazaki, and Makoto Sato, who called themselves the "Seven Bridge Buddies". Even when working on different pictures, they would meet at 12 noon and play Seven Bridge (a card game) in a Tatami room at Toho, with Jun Tazaki keeping score (Natsuki in Ezawa, 2016, 88). In *Dogora*, Natsuki plays Inspector Komai, a role very similar to Detective Shindo in *Ghidorah* but played with less self-assuredness.

Akiko Wakabayashi plays one of the diamond gangsters in *Dogora*. She originally wanted to be an artist but auditioned for Senkichi Taniguchi's *Uminari* (*Skyquake*) at Toho out of curiosity. Though the film was never made, Toho asked if she was interested in acting and signed her during the summer of her senior high-school year. Her screen debut came with *Song for a Bride* (1958), directed by Ishiro Honda. Her first film experience was actually in a scene shot for *A Holiday in Tokyo* (1958, Kajiro Yamamoto), but it was released after Honda's film (Wakabayashi in Tanobe, 2011a, 88–89). As her career developed, Wakabayashi's resumé spanned science fiction, comedies, Toho's International Secret Police series, an Italian comedy, and a turn as a "Bond Girl" opposite Sean Connery via *You Only Live Twice* (1967, Lewis Gilbert).

Originally, Kumi Mizuno was set to play Princess Salno in *Ghidorah*, announced as such via the October 1964 meeting of Toho's branch presidents; her name is also mentioned in a copy of the film's second script draft kept by the crew. Mizuno was no stranger to Toho special effects films, having starred in *Gorath* (1962, Ishiro Honda), *Matango* (1963, Ishiro Honda), and several Godzilla films that would follow. However, Wakabayashi replaced her as Salno by the time Ishiro Honda's drama unit began shooting on 16 October 1964 (Suzuki in Kimura, 2023, 85).

Hiroshi Koizumi plays almost the same role in *Ghidorah* as he did in *Dogora* and *Mothra vs. Godzilla*. In the latter, he was Dr. Miura, a scientist investigating Mothra's egg; in *Ghidorah*, he plays Dr. Murai, a scientist examining King Ghidorah's meteorite. Koizumi began his career as a radio announcer for NHK before joining Toho's New Face acting class in 1951. He debuted as a film actor the following year and signed a contract with Toho, appearing in dozens of films as the industry hit its second golden age. For example, in the same year he appeared in *Godzilla Raids Again*, Koizumi starred in ten other features in leading or supporting roles (Galbraith, 1996, 34; Homenick, 2017).

Much like *Dogora*, *Ghidorah*'s first script draft sees a criminal gang at its centre. Princess Salno is notably absent, and in her place is a smuggler named Goro Aikawa. Detective Shindo is a narcotics agent chasing the syndicate to which Aikawa belongs.

As in the finished film, the story opens with a UFO club gathered on a rooftop watching for flying saucers. Goro Aikawa bursts in, chased by Shindo. He falls from the roof just as a meteor shower illuminates the area. The following morning, he is found in the mountains by Professor Murai, close to King Ghidorah's crashed meteorite. Regaining consciousness, Aikawa says he is a Venusian. He also predicts the return of Rodan and Godzilla, the latter of which destroys the smugglers' ship (Kaneda, 2018, 218–19).

King Ghidorah's presence in this draft is of particular interest. It is described as having "a horn on its dragon-like head, with [a] sharp beak, and [a] Griffin-like body, and giant wings" (Asai in Ishii & Hirai, 2012, 88). In the finished film, we learn that King Ghidorah destroyed all life on Venus centuries ago, but this first draft makes the monster's threat less abstract. Shindo suggests using all of Earth's nuclear weapons against King Ghidorah, but Aikawa explains that although it may work, "the strong radiation will destroy every single life form on the Earth. Venus was destroyed in that manner. Venus' science was much more advanced than that of Earth. But science cannot defeat King Ghidorah" (Kaneda, 2018, 219–20). As the story develops, the United Nations plans to launch a nuclear strike against King Ghidorah, which Japan opposes. Not only does this attach a more specific threat to King Ghidorah, echoing the fate of Venus, but it positions the monster as a symbolic tool. In this draft, the monster's arrival upsets the precarious balance of nuclear weapon usage – an idea that would eventually feature in a Godzilla film via *The Return of Godzilla* (1984, Koji Hashimoto).

Another difference between the first draft and the finished film is that Aikawa suggests the alliance of the monsters instead of the Shobijin, though Mothra still argues with Godzilla and Rodan about uniting (Kaneda, 2018, 220). The climax of the first draft sees further differences: a mother asks Shindo and Naoko for help when her son is trapped at the bottom of a ravine. Aikawa is lowered down and manages to save the boy but is overwhelmed by falling rocks from the monster battle above. Shindo then saves Aikawa, who regains his senses (Sekizawa in Kimura, 2023, 113).

Also featured were ideas about Venusian-human integration and the potential to revive Venusian powers in humans (Kaneda, 2018, 220). A key alteration is the title itself. The front page of the first draft still has the final title, *Three Giant Monsters: The Greatest Battle on Earth*, but within the script itself is written *Four Monsters – The Biggest Battle in Earth History* (Asai in Ishii & Hirai, 2012, 88; Suzuki in Kimura, 2023, 83).

Sekizawa's second script draft is dated 26 September 1964, with the story closer to the finished film. Aikawa was replaced with Princess Salno, pursued by a gang of assassins trying to kill her. The threat of nuclear attack against King Ghidorah was scaled back, suggested only as a last-minute defence, much as in the finished film. Although the smugglers and Shindo's associated investigation were removed, traces of *Dogora* still remain – not least with Yosuke Natsuki's casting and role as a detective. In fact, it was between the first and second script drafts that Natsuki had been listed as part of the cast at Toho's monthly meeting of its branch presidents on 7 September (Suzuki in Kimura, 2023, 83–84).

The third and final script is dated 7 October 1964. Few changes had been made from the second draft, but elements were polished and clarified. For example, an explanation for Salno's miraculous escape from her exploding plane was included, delivered by the UFO club leader discussing dimensional shifts (Suzuki in Kimura, 2023, 85). The final draft still features many elements not included in the eventual film. For example, in all three script drafts, King Ghidorah was set to ravage New York City. In the final script, Sekizawa wrote the monster's assault on America as follows:

King Ghidorah appears in the sky above the Statue of Liberty.

A sharp beam of light shoots out from his foot.

The building it hits floats up into mid-air and suddenly breaks apart.

Boats float up near the cliff.

> The sea water is whipped up like a tornado.
>
> The sea water and boats are dropped on central Manhattan like the bottom falling out of a container.
>
> The large boats force themselves between tightly packed buildings.
>
> The water rains down incessantly like a waterfall.
>
> Balanced and unbalanced phenomenon appear alternately in a scene of mayhem that has never been seen before.
>
> Finally, the Statue of Liberty too is attacked by King Ghidorah.
>
> For an instant the Statue of Liberty is shown in photo negative.
>
> Before our eyes, the Statue of Liberty is reduced to fine powder like flour, little more than tree leaves, and with one blow slowly crumbles.
>
> A strange sound echoes from King Ghidorah as he takes off into the sky and flies around like a storm.

Another connection across all three script drafts is how Sekizawa describes King Ghidorah's devastation. As seen here, the monster's powers are written in particularly fantastic fashion, detailing far more surreal destruction than that which features in the finished film. Although scenes of New York were set to be shot in late November/early December (according to a production schedule dated 20 October), the sequence was ultimately never produced (Suzuki in Kimura, 2023, 85–86). However, traces remain in the film's lobby card set, one of which is a mock-up of King Ghidorah next to the Statue of Liberty.

Additionally, at the end of the third script draft, the military contemplate how to deal with Godzilla and Rodan after King Ghidorah has retreated. However, the Shobijin explain that by the time mankind has found a way, the monsters will be gone. As written, the last scene featured Godzilla and Rodan disappearing into the deep fog surrounding Mount Fuji.

More Cast Members and Production Stories

Akiko Wakabayashi's own wardrobe came in handy for *Ghidorah*. Used to wearing what she called a "boy's style", Wakabayashi was spotted by Honda on the Toho lot wearing jeans and a man's hat. Honda was enthusiastic about the look and it became Salno's attire when under Venusian control. For her possessed state, Wakabayashi avoided direct eye contact with her co-stars, playing the part as if sleepwalking (Wakabayashi in Tanobe, 2011a, 91). When the Venusians possess her at the film's beginning, Wakabayashi was temporarily blinded when a light was aimed directly at her eyes to depict the possession.

While working on *Ghidorah*, Wakabayashi was appearing in other projects, and it was physically taking its toll. She was so tired during production that she fell asleep on the bed in Tsukamoto's laboratory. She would later recall,

> I was actually sleeping through most of the time because I had to stay up all night the night before for filming of a TV show. I was working on a different project at the same time. So, during the actual filming, I was really sleeping, and I didn't wake up till way after the filming was done. When I finally woke up, I asked Mr. Honda, "Why didn't you wake me up?". Mr. Honda said, "Because someone told me that you were up all night for the other show." (Wakabayashi in Ezawa, 2016, 134)

Of the production team, Wakabayashi would say it was like a family unit with Honda as the father (Wakabayashi in Ezawa, 2016, 138). Honda's inspiration for her character is of particular interest. Wakabayashi was directed to play her final scene (her tearful goodbye at the airport) like Audrey Hepburn in *Roman Holiday* (1953, William Wyler). The similarity is firm: both Princess Ann (Hepburn) and Princess Salno say an emotional goodbye to their companion/protector at an official event, their feelings stifled by formality. More than just the ending, *Ghidorah* shares multiple similarities with *Roman Holiday*: a princess from a fictional nation is abroad in a foreign country; the male lead identifies the princess through a newspaper photograph; the princesses ditch their formal attire for a casual look; the male lead accompanies the princess and knows who she really is; and the princesses are pursued by grim-faced men in suits.

The role of reporter Naoko would be Yuriko Hoshi's second turn as a journalist in a Godzilla film after Junko in *Mothra vs. Godzilla*. But while Junko was under the wing of Akira Takarada's Sakai, Naoko in *Ghidorah* works with greater autonomy. Hoshi started her career as a teenager with the Takarazuka Revue, an all-women theatrical troupe established in 1913 by one of Toho's founding organisers, Ichizo Kobayashi (Anderson & Richie, 1982, 236; Yomota, 2019, 14). Although she initially turned down an offer to stay at Toho during a visit, Hoshi eventually joined the studio and would become a regular in the company's popular "Young Guy" series for young adults (Galbraith, 1998, 46; Galbraith, 1996, 19).

According to *Ghidorah*'s theatrical programme book, Hoshi prepared to play a reporter by going out and interviewing strangers. She explained:

> Up till this film, my parts were mostly as office girls, so a leading career woman was a very attractive character to me. However, I could not think of anyone that I could use as a model, so I was having a hard time imagining how I should play my part.

With her own portable tape recorder, Hoshi headed to the main street leading to the Yoyogi General Sports Complex, a busy area given the recent Tokyo Olympics. She began interviewing police who were on patrol, asking them about the security status of the area; some of them believed she was a real reporter. She also interviewed foreign nationals to meet the "international mood" of the film.

Other cast members include twin sisters Emi and Yumi Ito, appearing as the Shobijin for the third and final time. The pair were discovered as teenagers whilst singing in a nightclub in Nagoya. Quickly signed to Watanabe Productions (a major talent agency) in Tokyo, the sisters began performing as The Peanuts, releasing their first single in 1959 – which was a major hit (Suzuki in Tanobe, 2011a, 58). Although their film career was fairly brief, Emi and Yumi Ito starred in several films beyond their Toho monster roles. However, as if signalling the end of The Peanuts' association with the Shobijin, *Ghidorah, the Three-Headed Monster* does not feature Yuji Koseki's famous Mothra song – first heard in *Mothra* and arranged acapella in *Mothra vs. Godzilla*. Instead, the pair sing a new piece ("Cry for Happiness") when calling for Mothra to fight King Ghidorah. Koseki's iconic piece would not reappear in the Godzilla series until 1992's *Godzilla vs. Mothra* (Takao Okawara).

Ghidorah, the Three-Headed Monster

The final key cast member was Hisaya Ito, playing the menacing lead assassin, Malmess. He started his acting career with Toei before joining Toho in 1957. Both before and after his turn in *Ghidorah*, Ito appeared in several genre pictures, including *The H-Man*, *Giant Monster Varan*, and *Atragon*; usually these were minor military, police, or scientific roles (Galbraith, 1996, 27). Originally, Yoshio Tsuchiya, an Akira Kurosawa regular who had played the lead invader in *The Mysterians*, had been considered to play Malmess – listed as such in *Ghidorah*'s final script draft and in the film's first shooting schedule. However, Tsuchiya had been working on Kurosawa's *Red Beard* (1965), which had encountered production difficulties and was delayed. As such, he could not appear in *Ghidorah* and Ito replaced him.

On this subject, Nobutaka Suzuki (in Kimura, 2023, 85–87) has clarified a long-repeated line (in both English-language and Japanese texts) that claims *Ghidorah* was put into production because *Red Beard* fell behind schedule. As Suzuki explains, it was announced at Toho's branch president meeting in early September 1964 that *Red Beard* would complete production by the end of the month, having already been pushed back from a planned June wrap and autumn release. At that point, *Ghidorah* was already well into pre-production, and we know that Tanaka had ideas for the film as early as April. Furthermore, *Red Beard* would continue to be delayed further, not seeing release until April 1965. It is unlikely that Tsuchiya would have been considered for *Ghidorah* if he was still working on a film whose delays supposedly put *Ghidorah* into production.

Ghidorah's monster scale was mirrored in its location photography, with scenes filmed at Mount Aso (from which Rodan emerges), Tokyo's Ueno Park (where Salno gives her first public warnings), Yokohama (where Godzilla comes ashore), Gotemba (near Mount Fuji where the final battle takes place), and Matsumoto (over which King Ghidorah flies after its fiery birth). While shooting in Matsumoto, assistant special effects director Teruyoshi Nakano recalled filming crowds reacting to King Ghidorah's incoming attack: "I was talking to them like, 'Hello, everybody, we are the location group from Toho! If you look up right now, there is a monster flying in the sky!' Then everybody looked up, so we just filmed it without telling them that filming had already started" (Nakano & Someya, 2007, 60; Ryfle & Godziszewski, 2017, 216).

Monster Costumes

The special effects for *Ghidorah, the Three-Headed Monster* were characterised much as they had been for previous Godzilla films: detailed miniature cities, elaborate monster costumes, precise optical work, and high-speed photography. The special effects for *Ghidorah* marked technical advances for the Godzilla series, revealing the dedication and ingenuity of Eiji Tsuburaya's effects personnel.

King Ghidorah was designed by Akira Watanabe, special effects art director for many of Toho's 1950s and 1960s special effects films. The monster draws from Yamata-no-Orochi – the eight-headed serpent of Japanese mythology – as well as the Hydra and Pegasus of Greek mythology (Ishii & Hirai, 2012, 89; Tanaka, 1983, 280). There is also speculation that King Ghidorah was inspired by the three-headed dragon that appears in *Ilya Muromets* (1956, Aleksandr Ptushko), a Soviet fantasy epic from Mosfilm that was released in Japan in 1959 (Takaki, 1998, 78; Ono & Iwahata, 2023, 5). In conversations with this author, Professor Daisuke Miyao has pointed out how the film was noteworthy in Japanese pop-cultural discourse. Famed manga artist Osamu Tezuka (creator of many influential works like *Astro Boy* and *Ambassador Magma*) co-authored an adaptation of *Ilya Muromets* in 1985 with science-fiction novelist Yasutaka Tsutsui. Given its impact on such figures, the film's possible influence on King Ghidorah is worth consideration.

According to future Godzilla series special effects director Koichi Kawakita, the enormous King Ghidorah suit weighed 80kg. When its necks were outstretched, it was three times the size of a person (Kawakita in Ishii & Hirai, 2012, 89). It was operated internally by Shoichi Hirose, nicknamed "Solomon" for having served in the Solomon Islands during the war. Unlike the relative range of movement enjoyed by Godzilla suit performer Haruo Nakajima, Hirose could do little more than crouch and grasp a crossbar in front of him for balance. He would operate the feet and legs while Ghidorah's necks, heads, wings, and tails were manipulated by wires.

Suit modeler Keizo Murase recalled King Ghidorah's construction during an interview with Brett Homenick (2018a):

> The skin was too heavy, so at first the suit actor was not able to move. So, some of King Ghidorah's body parts were moved with piano wire, so many staff members

had to operate the piano wire at the same time. The piano wire had to be on in three places on the head in order to move it: the back of the head, the forehead, and the top of the back. To move the head side-to-side, piano wire was attached to the left and right cheeks.

The wire operation for King Ghidorah proved most challenging. Special effects technician Fumio Nakadai recalled Ghidorah needing about six operators in total: one for the wings, three for the necks (depending on the type of movement), and one or two for the tails. "It sounds ridiculous, but only a real human could've made the realistic movement" (Nakadai in Tanaka, 1983, 286). Special effects cinematographer Sadamasa Arikawa also noted that "the heads would get tangled, the piano wires would shine and show up on film or get caught between the scales, it was really a hell of a job. How the whole army of wire workers got up on the rafters and crowded together looked like circus acrobats" (Arikawa in Tanaka, 1983, 286).

Haruo Nakajima, playing Godzilla for the fifth time in *Ghidorah*, remembered King Ghidorah's wireworks posing a challenge for the climactic battle. Speaking in his autobiography, Nakajima recalled,

> [King Ghidorah's] appearance was flashy indeed, but he was huge, and with so many wires, it had no mobile flexibility at all. He was definitely a troublesome opponent to deal with. Except for minor movements that the actor inside could make, Ghidorah wasn't able to do anything. Godzilla was the one to attack, get hit, chase, get bopped, etc., everything was Godzilla playing solo. On top of it, the wires controlling his necks got caught by Godzilla and snapped. It was so much trouble! (Nakajima, 2010, 141)

Despite these issues, King Ghidorah's execution marks a technical development from Tsuburaya's realisation of the actual Yamata-no-Orochi five years earlier in *The Three Treasures* (1959, Hiroshi Inagaki), itself another intensive wirework operation.

King Ghidorah's colour scheme changed as production went on. The suit was first produced with a blue hue for the body and a rainbow scheme for the wings. While Keizo Murase (Homenick, 2018a) has said the suit was always gold (as in the finished film), and that the blue colouration was simply a result of how the material looked when drying, special effects script co-ordinator Keiko Suzuki remembers seeing the suit in the original blue/green colouration. In fact, it was Suzuki herself who suggested that Ghidorah be changed to gold. She later recalled,

> When I was told that King Ghidorah was done and it was just getting dried off, I went to see it. There was King Ghidorah hanging from the ceiling, kind of a greenish colour that sort of looked like Anguirus. When I saw that, I told Mr. Tsuburaya, who was standing just by me, that I thought King Ghidorah should be gold since it is coming from Venus. In my mind, if it were coming from Venus, it would be coming from the light. I didn't think it would be a dark tone like that. Then Mr. Tsuburaya looked like he was thinking for a while, and then he went to the suit makers. I went with him. He said to [Teizo] Toshimitsu, "I regret to say this, Toshimitsu, but can you change the colour to gold?" (Suzuki in Tanobe, 2011b, 96)

As well as the enormous suit, smaller King Ghidorah models were constructed for flying scenes and long shots. One of the largest flying models was one metre in length and proved just as difficult to operate. Special effects technician Koji Matsumoto said "we hung it from a crane or something and made it only so the wings would move. For the necks, we made them move alternately, and attached two wires" (Matsumoto in Tanaka, 1983, 284).

While these smaller models were employed for scenes of King Ghidorah in flight, the full-sized suit was still used for take-off. As Fumio Nakadai noted, Hirose was not in the suit for these take-off shots. "We used the big one up to the take off, and then switched to the smaller one" (Nakadai in Tanaka, 1983, 285). Koji Matsumoto added that "making the actual one fly was a heck of a job. We hung it from a monorail, but it was so heavy. There were people above [in the rafters], and if they fall, they're gonna die. We moved all the necks, and the wings too. We only could film one cut per day at the time" (Matsumoto in Tanaka, 1983, 285).

The film's other flying monster, Rodan, received an updated design and was performed by Koji Uruki. For its first appearance since 1956, Rodan's suit was given a more comical look. Rodan's eyes were made rounder and could be moved via remote control, appearing more human than the reptilian look from its debut film. Additionally, the monster's neck was elongated, allowing for greater movement. Several Rodan models and puppets were also produced at different scales. Marking a technical development over its original appearance, Rodan's flight model was able to flap its wings – unlike the elegant but simple gliding motion of the 1956 version (Tanaka, 1983, 283). Two puppets of Rodan were produced which could be manually operated for close-ups: a full-body version manipulated with rods, and an upper-body model controlled like a hand puppet (Asai in Ishii & Hirai, 2012, 89; Tanaka, 1983, 283).

Godzilla similarly received a 60cm puppet, fitted with an aerosol spray for its atomic breath. Both the Godzilla and Rodan puppets were used extensively for *Ghidorah*, allowing for several close-ups as the two monsters brawl near Mount Fuji. The full Godzilla suit was functionally the same as the one used in *Mothra vs. Godzilla*. However, its head was modified, and the eyes were renovated to accommodate remote control. Like Rodan, Godzilla's eyes appear much more human than in previous films.

Performing as Godzilla was a difficult task for Haruo Nakajima, who remembered,

> It wasn't easy, for real. Once filming started, for two to three months I didn't feel like eating lunch. If I could, maybe soup, that was it. It could be because the smell of the suit was so overwhelming. So, I tried to eat enough breakfast every day. Also, I tried to get enough sleep. After the day was over, I took a bath and had a drink. (Nakajima, 2010, 139–40)

Nakajima also recalled that *Ghidorah*'s special effects were shot on Toho's Stage 11, which was built in 1962 specifically for special effects shooting. Stage 11 possessed a higher horizon than Stage 8 – which, along with Stage 9, had been constructed for special effects shooting in 1955 for *Godzilla Raids Again* (Tanaka, 1991, 62). This meant that Stage 11 could accommodate the enormous Mount Fuji background painting. As sound would be added in post-production for special effects scenes, Stage 11 dispensed with soundproofing. However, its thinner ceiling and walls meant it quickly warmed up during summertimes, adding to the intense heat of the lighting. Comically (and unsurprisingly), Nakajima noted how much he would sweat in the Godzilla suit. In turn, performing as Godzilla would cure him if he had been drinking: "being in Godzilla was definitely the silver bullet for a hangover" (Nakajima, 2010, 140).

Lastly, Mothra was not performed by any actor for *Ghidorah*. Rather, the mechanical larval Mothra props from *Mothra vs. Godzilla* were reused. One of them was self-propelled while the other was designed for wire operation (Asai in Ishii & Hirai, 2012, 89).

Optical Work

The optical work for *Ghidorah, the Three-Headed Monster* was more extensive than that for any prior Toho monster film. Optical illustrator Sadao Iizuka remembered the film having a staggering 240 cuts, more than anything he had worked on (Iizuka & Matsumoto, 2016, 160). With his background in art, Iizuka had previously worked in various part-time roles in the special effects art department for films like *Godzilla* and *Godzilla Raids Again*. Eiji Tsuburaya eventually took Iizuka under his wing and tasked him with inserting animation into live-action footage. Without prior knowledge in the field of optical work, Iizuka nonetheless took up the challenge through experimentation and trial and error. Eventually, Iizuka hit his stride by hand-drawing beams, lasers, and other optical effects, which were composited into live-action material. By the mid-1960s, Iizuka's contract with Toho had him working on three films per year (Homenick, 2021).

Iizuka's most striking contribution to *Ghidorah* is King Ghidorah's fiery birth. The monster erupts from its meteorite, bathed in overlapping explosions as flames outline its shape. Keiko Suzuki recalled the original idea coming from a conversation she had with Tsuburaya, taking inspiration from a 1947 Soviet animated film called *The Humpbacked Horse* (I. Ivano-Vano), which features several firebirds that glow and pulse with light. In a 2023 interview, Suzuki remembered,

> On my way back from seeing the newly painted gold [King Ghidorah] with Mr. Tsuburaya, he muttered, "I wonder what we should do about the scene where the monster shows up." I mentioned how in my mind, I thought it would resemble a particular Soviet animated film featuring a phoenix. He nodded his assent and went to the staff room, where he drew a quick storyboard and showed it to Sadao Iizuka and proposed that setup for the scene. I just happened to be watching a lot

of movies as a bystander and made these passing comments. (Suzuki in Ono & Iwahata, 2023, 33)

Iizuka then developed the idea and added his own stamp, later recalling his inspirations and work process for the sequence:

> First, there was the birth of King Ghidorah. For this, [Tsuburaya] plain said, "I want Ghidorah to be born from a fireball". So, originally I just made it like King Ghidorah shows up in the explosion, just by overlapping. But that only looked like fire was just burning, and it wasn't interesting at all. Then we decided to add a little more detail and came up with that kind of contour. I got an idea from, you know, there was the thing called the "Monster from the Id" in *Forbidden Planet* (1956 [Fred M. Wilcox]), right? I got a hint from the animation of those outlines. I watched it a few years ago and I liked how those things showed up like "veeev, veeev, veeev!" from nothing. (Iizuka & Matsumoto, 2016, 160)

Tsuburaya was receptive to Iizuka's idea and the effect was achieved with an airbrush. Iizuka also painstakingly reversed frames to produce the effect's unique movement: "It was a lot of work. Start the frame as one, two, three.... And when it came to the eighth frame, put it back to six, then go to eight again. It was really a tedious job" (Iizuka & Matsumoto, 2016, 161). Tedious though it may have been to produce, King Ghidorah's birth has become a highlight of the Godzilla series, replicated and reused many times in later films.

Iizuka also created the "gravity beams" that King Ghidorah liberally zaps out. Originally, Tsuburaya had envisioned Ghidorah breathing fire, but this was dropped when he and Iizuka saw the monster's heads thrashing about in the rushes. Instead, Iizuka proposed electrical discharges because the direction of Ghidorah's heads would be less important. Incorporated into the animation was Iizuka's three-frame idea: leaving three frames when a beam hits an object before it explodes. Iizuka's thinking was that, in previous films, beams simply hit their targets and they blew up. By leaving just a few frames before the explosion, it gave the impression that the beam was having an effect on its target *before* it exploded (Iizuka & Matsumoto, 2016, 162–63).

Sadao Iizuka's optical work for King Ghidorah's fiery birth. *Ghidorah, the Three-Headed Monster.* Producer: Tomoyuki Tanaka. Director: Ishiro Honda.

It should be mentioned that the original fire effect for King Ghidorah is somewhat depicted in the film's promotional material. However, as Iizuka explained, "the reason why the actual film and those stills for ads were different was because there was a professional 'stillman' who only did the ads".

Miniatures

Numerous miniatures were constructed for *Ghidorah*. Some depicted urban environments like Yokohama, while others showed natural spaces around Kurobe Dam where King Ghidorah's meteorite lands. All were built with precise attention to detail.

Assistant special effects art director Yasuyuki Inoue was Eiji Tsuburaya's right-hand man, designing the miniature sets for *Ghidorah* as he had for all prior Godzilla films. Inoue served during the war but lost his right foot and was sent home. Speaking in the 2007 documentary, *Bringing Godzilla Down to Size*, Inoue explained that it was difficult to find work when he was discharged in January 1946. Entering a vocational school for injured veterans, Inoue learned to make furniture; he would eventually major in furniture design at Nippon University.

Inoue's furniture work influenced his film career tremendously. His models found him

Ghidorah, the Three-Headed Monster

work at Shintoho in 1953 (a studio formed as a breakaway from Toho following strike action in the late 1940s, hence its name, which means "New Toho"), and he would be loaned out to Toho in 1954 for *Godzilla*. He would go on to become supervisor of Toho's special effects art department.

When working on a project like *Ghidorah*, Inoue would receive the script and create an overall look for the project. A staff meeting would follow, and Inoue would present his blueprints to Tsuburaya, who would say where he wanted the monsters to appear. Models would then be constructed which Tsuburaya examined to plan out the direction of a scene. Finally, the art department would build a full miniature set over the course of two-to-three weeks. Recalling *Ghidorah*'s production, Inoue explained,

> When I first read the script, I thought it was very interesting. So, when I made the sets, my mindset was to recreate the real places, not just make miniatures for the monsters to destroy. As a result, I was very satisfied with what we made, especially with how the Yokohama sets turned out. (Inoue in Aoki, 2012, 115)

The Yokohama sets are indeed impressive. The Yokohama Marine Tower was recreated in perfect detail for King Ghidorah's aerial attack. Comparing photographs of the real tower in the 1960s to the miniature version reveals how diligently Inoue and his staff worked. Fitted with explosives, the tower collapses after it is struck by Sadao Iizuka's gravity beams, its weight accentuated by high-speed photography.

The same can be said for the Yokohama port area, including Yamashita Park, which was meticulously recreated in miniature for Godzilla's landing. Inoue's design sketches illustrate his precision in recreating real spaces on screen. As the port's geography remains mostly unchanged as of this writing, side-by-side comparisons emphasise the skill Inoue brought to *Ghidorah*.

Speaking in NHK's 2014 documentary, *Godzilla's 60th Anniversary: The Amazing World of Japanese Special Effects*, Jiro Shirasaki, one of Inoue's apprentices, explained that "[Inoue] was serious about his work, always starting with collecting research material, no matter the film. From there, he worked diligently to recreate the real thing just as it was".

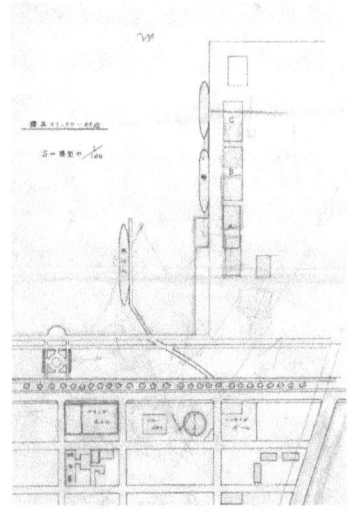

Yasuyuki Inoue's original design sketch for the Yokohama port area where Godzilla comes ashore. Used with generous permission from Toyomi Togo.

Yamashita Park, Yokohama, as of 2022. Image taken from Google Maps.

As Inoue explained in *Bringing Godzilla Down to Size*, "I don't think of my sets as miniatures. Shooting on my set is like shooting on the actual location". Assistant art director Toshiro Aoki echoed this sentiment, explaining that staff members "trained [themselves] to observe the real world" so that it could be recreated exactly.

Under Tsuburaya's leadership, artists like Inoue worked to create an authentic sense of reality on screen through the special effects. The thought process behind

Ghidorah, the Three-Headed Monster

Sadao Iizuka's "three-frame idea" similarly suggests a pursuit of reality in the work. This is partly why the more playful development of Godzilla's appearance and characterisation in this and subsequent films works, because the world the monsters inhabit (both in terms of Tsuburaya's effects and in Honda's direction of the actors) has a consistent atmosphere and reality captured by artists like Inoue.

In an essay penned for *Terror of Mechagodzilla*'s programme booklet in 1975, director Ishiro Honda summarised the approach:

> [Special effects] techniques are mere trickeries and not actually real. But it is our job to make it look as if they are real to the audience, so it is very important for the director to have the attitude as if he is actually standing in that scene himself. A giant Godzilla standing 50 metres in height suddenly appears in front of you. Oh my goodness, what are we to do! It is necessary for the director to actually feel this sense of shock and surprise. When real things are filmed in its natural state, we call these documentary films. [Special effects] films are fundamentally the same as documentary films, in that although the objects filmed are miniatures, it is done with the feeling that what is seen through the lens is actually real, in tens of times the size.

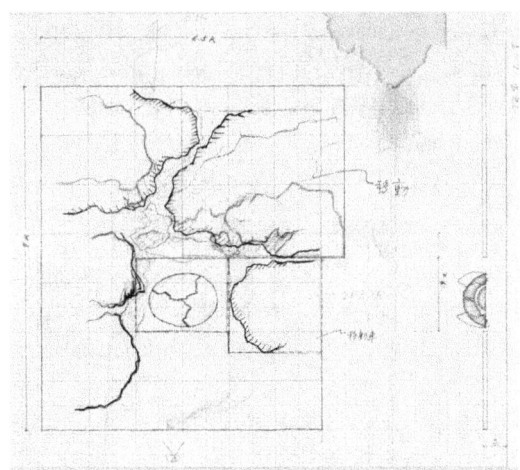

Yasuyuki Inoue's original design sketch for King Ghidorah's meteorite. Used with generous permission from Toyomi Togo.

CONSTELLATIONS

Japanese Theatrical Releases

Ghidorah, the Three-Headed Monster was released in Japan on 20 December 1964, selling 4,320,000 tickets (Ryfle, 1998, 310) and earning ¥375 million (Ryfle & Godziszewski, 2017, 217). Its co-feature was *Hana no Oedo Musekinin* (roughly translated as *Irresponsibility of the Great Edo*), directed by Kajiro Yamamoto – Ishiro Honda's mentor.

Specifically, *Irresponsibility of the Great Edo* was a part of a series of "Irresponsibility" comedy films similar to Toho's *Shacho* (or "Company President") salaryman comedies. The Irresponsibility series was a vehicle for the Crazy Cats, a popular comic musical group who featured in dozens of films, most often with Hitoshi Ueki and Hajime Hana (Galbraith, 1996, 15, 77; Yomota, 2019, 129–30). *Irresponsibility of the Great Edo* was a period comedy in which Ueki plays a skilled fighter (and ladies' man) who travels to Edo to avenge his father's death.

While there could often be variety within double bills at the time anyway, *Ghidorah*'s co-feature nonetheless illustrates the wide audience Godzilla films still courted at the time. This is also emphasised by *Mothra vs. Godzilla*'s co-feature: a black-and-white war film called *Operation Antlion* (1964, Takashi Tsuboshima), part of Toho's "Desperados" series. Produced by Tomoyuki Tanaka, written by Shinichi Sekizawa, and featuring many familiar faces (including Akihiko Hirata, Jun Tazaki, and *Ghidorah*'s Yosuke Natsuki), *Operation Antlion* is about six Japanese soldiers chosen to destroy a bridge to prevent enemy forces from advancing – worlds apart from the colourful thrills of *Mothra vs. Godzilla*.

Films like *Irresponsibility of the Great Edo* and *Operation Antlion* tell us two things. Firstly, their cast and crew reinforce an argument made by Stuart Galbraith IV (1998, 12), that only when one considers the enormity of the Japanese film industry at the time can we understand how actors and crew easily stepped between multiple genres and productions at once. Secondly, the wide appeal of these co-features illustrates that Godzilla films still maintained a broad audience at the time.

In turn, it is arguable that *Ghidorah* was one of the last Godzilla films in the original series to court the widest audience possible. The Irresponsibility film it was paired with undoubtedly held broad appeal because of the Crazy Cats' popularity. Older viewers may have similarly been more familiar with the film's kabuki and folklore references. At the same time, Haruo Nakajima was appearing in the Godzilla suit for publicity events at department stores, entertaining crowds of enthralled children (Nakajima, 2010, 146). *Ghidorah* also sold the highest number of tickets in the decade after *King Kong vs. Godzilla* (Ryfle, 1998, 310), likely helped by its release in the lucrative New Year period.

Significantly, Toho's November 1964 press sheet stressed the film's broad appeal in its instructions for exhibitors:

> Monster movies have a wide demographic appeal, with fans from children to adults. Ensure that the product does not come across as too cheap or kiddie. This is intended to be a true entertainment product that grown adults can enjoy in their own right. It should be fun for the whole family; the goal is bringing the entire family unit out to see the picture. (Suzuki in Kimura, 2023, 86)

By comparison, the next few Godzilla films would slowly begin playing to narrower audiences, with cinema attendance decreasing slightly for the following year's *Invasion of Astro-Monster* (1965, Ishiro Honda), and then again for 1966's *Ebirah, Horror of the Deep* (Jun Fukuda) and subsequent sequels. Furthermore, the general makeup of the audience gradually became much younger.

This shift would ultimately coincide with the decline of the Japanese film industry. The studios could no longer keep up the pace they had once pursued, and television had hit the industry hard by the end of the 1960s. Many of Toho's profitable film series (like the above-mentioned *Shacho* movies) were over by the 1970s. Other major studios were similarly affected: Daiei went bankrupt in 1971, while Nikkatsu shifted its output to "Roman Porno" adult films entirely. The number of films each studio made was greatly reduced, with the majors putting out just 163 in 1974, compared to 277 ten years prior. The total number of cinemas in Japan also dropped from 4,927 in 1964 to 2,468 in 1974 (Kitaura in Fujiki & Phillips, 2020, 121–22; Galbraith, 1996, 467–68).

CONSTELLATIONS

Amidst this industry upheaval, Toei would once again influence Toho. Earlier in the 1960s, Toei had launched a series of children's entertainment events to coincide with the school holidays, screening animated movies, an assortment of TV episodes, and shorts. These festivals went by several names, including the Toei Children's Festival in the spring of 1967 and the Toei Manga Parade in the summer of 1968, eventually settling on the Toei Manga Festival by the spring of 1969.

In response to Toei's first Great Manga Parade in summer 1964, Toho reissued *King Kong vs. Godzilla* at Toho-contracted theatres on 25 July (Suzuki in Kimura, 2023, 81–82). Likely in further competition, Toho's monster films in the latter half of the 1960s were increasingly shown in the summertime with films aimed squarely at children. For example, *War of the Gargantuas* (1966, Ishiro Honda) was shown with *Jungle Emperor* (1966, Eiichi Yamamoto), an anime feature compiled of episodes from the 1965–66 series of the same name – itself an adaptation of Osamu Tezuka's 1950–54 manga. *King Kong Escapes* (1967, Ishiro Honda) was similarly shown with *Feature Monster Movie: Ultraman* (1967, Hajime Tsuburaya), another compilation film featuring several episodes of Tsuburaya Productions' family-oriented *Ultraman* (1966–67) television series.

Then, in December 1969, Toho held its first Toho Champion Festival, properly replicating Toei's formula. Until 1978, the Champion Festival would be held two or three times a year in spring, summer, and winter to line up with the school holiday periods. With the increasingly younger crowd courted by Toho's science-fiction pictures, the Toho Champion Festival consolidated and affirmed the new makeup of Godzilla's audience.

New Godzilla films made between 1969 and 1975 were released directly through the Toho Champion Festival. These Godzilla films were paired with anime features and episodes of Tsuburaya Productions' latest superhero shows like *Mirrorman* and *Return of Ultraman* (both 1971–72). The Champion Festivals also reissued older Toho titles as well, trimmed to just over an hour to focus on monster action. Such reissues included *Mothra*, *Mothra vs. Godzilla*, and *Ghidorah, the Three-Headed Monster*.

Ghidorah was reissued for the Champion Festival on 12 December 1971. It was screened alongside *Terror of the Tornado Monsters* (episodes 13 and 14 of *Return of Ultraman* edited together), episode 74 of TV anime *The Adventures of Hutch the Honeybee*, two episodes of TV anime *Inakappe Taisho* (which roughly translates to *The Hick Boss*), and a short called *The Little Match Girl*. *Ghidorah*'s Japanese title was also altered slightly for this release, changed from *Three Giant Monsters: The Greatest Battle on Earth* to *Godzilla, Mothra, King Ghidorah: The Greatest Battle on Earth* (Nakamura & Hazawa, 2014, 42–43).

For its Champion Festival reissue, *Ghidorah* was shortened from 93 minutes to 73, removing some scenes in their entirety and trimming others; Ishiro Honda handled the re-edit himself. Interestingly, some of the Champion edits mirror those made for *Ghidorah*'s US release in 1965. The US release and its changes will be discussed in Chapter Four, but for now it is worth highlighting the similar edits Honda implemented. For example, in the original 1964 version, when we cut to the police station at the film's beginning, Shindo has a brief conversation with a reporter about strange recent happenings before the chief arrives. In both the US and Champion cuts, that contextual conversation is excised, and we go straight into Shindo's talk with the chief. Later, when Salno is making her warnings at Ueno Park, the Champion cut removes most of the spectators' heckling and cuts straight to Naoko's questions; the US version similarly trims the heckling but to a lesser degree. Both versions also delete a brief scene in which Naoko meets with her colleagues to discuss their *Mystery in the 20th Century* series.

As will be discussed in Chapter Four, *Ghidorah*'s US distributor was certainly aware of the film's appeal to children (as shown by the marketing ploys in its press book). The fact that some of its edits were also implemented for the Champion version – which was directly aimed at children – suggests their effectiveness in preparing the film for its American release.

Chapter Three: Interpreting *Ghidorah, the Three-Headed Monster*

Even in its earliest drafts, Shinichi Sekizawa's script for *Ghidorah, the Three-Headed Monster* featured an alliance between Godzilla, Rodan, and Mothra. That alliance, and its depiction of the monsters as heroic, offers myriad ways to interpret the film: it positions *Ghidorah* as the culmination of themes from the prior Mothra films; it furthers Godzilla's character development; and it offers a reflection of Japan's curated image in 1964. This chapter offers an exploration of these ideas.

Our first examination is to consider *Ghidorah* as the final chapter in a loose thematic trilogy. *Mothra*, *Mothra vs. Godzilla*, and *Ghidorah* exhibit numerous continuities. As with most Toho monster films of the era, these titles largely possess the same crew and many returning cast members. Some characters reappear directly (e.g., the Shobijin) while others are functionally the same as their predecessors (e.g., Hiroshi Koizumi as Professor Chujo, Professor Miura, and Professor Murai). We can also see ideas reappearing across Sekizawa's scripts for all three films. Trust, co-operation, and connection are recurrent themes. In each film, we see trust between individuals, groups, and even nations being broken, repaired, or developed. It begins with relative simplicity in *Mothra*, with the broken trust between Japan and the Shobijin embodied by Mothra's rampage. It takes a more complicated form in *Mothra vs. Godzilla*, in which connection between peoples is left unresolved. Finally, in *Ghidorah*, trust can be seen between the monsters themselves, facilitating part of their symbolic and character transformations.

Thematic Continuities across *Mothra*, *Mothra vs. Godzilla*, and *Ghidorah, the Three-Headed Monster*

In *Mothra*, an expedition is mounted to Infant Island, a land which bore the brunt of atomic testing. Financed by Clark Nelson (Jerry Ito), a seedy entrepreneur from the fictional nation of Rolisica (the country responsible for the atomic tests), the expedition finds a jungle paradise beyond the island's harsh exterior. During their exploration, Professor Chujo (Hiroshi Koizumi) becomes ensnared by a bloodsucking plant. He is rescued by two tiny women: the Shobijin (Emi and Yumi Ito), supernatural conduits for Infant Island's monster god, Mothra. The Shobijin's goodwill is repaid with treachery when Nelson and his henchmen return to kidnap them and massacre the islanders. Back in Japan, Nelson puts the twins on display, unaware that the song they sing is a call to Mothra. Professor Chujo, tenacious reporter Zenichiro "snapping turtle" Fukuda (Frankie Sakai), and photographer Michi (Kyoko Kagawa) try to convince Nelson to free the twins and return them to their island. Nelson refuses, and Mothra destroys much of Tokyo in her search for the Shobijin, eventually constructing a chrysalis on Tokyo Tower. Although protective of Nelson at first, Rolisica eventually sends atomic heat cannons to help Japan, but they simply awaken the adult Mothra. Nelson escapes with the Shobijin to Rolisica's New Kirk City but Mothra follows. The Rolisican authorities find and shoot Nelson before painting Infant Island's Mothra symbol on an airport runway. Mothra is calmed, and the Shobijin return home.

Immediately, goodwill and faith are shown by the Shobijin when they save Chujo. Clark Nelson's greed betrays that trust, and the betrayal is embodied by Mothra's spectacular rampage.

Nelson belongs to Rolisica, a fictional amalgam of Russia and the United States, though it more evidently stands in for the latter. Its place in the narrative is significant, providing space for both historical reflection and for trust and co-operation to emerge as themes.

As mentioned in Chapter One, *Mothra* originally existed in serialised form as *The Luminous Fairies and Mothra*. It was written by Shinichiro Nakamura, Takehiko Fukunaga, and Yoshie Hotta and was published in the *Weekly Asahi Extra* in early 1961. Nakamura was asked by Hideyuki Shiino (Tomoyuki Tanaka's assistant) to write the story during the summer of 1960, and so he reached out to Fukunaga and Hotta to collaborate; each would pen a chapter. The significance of Rolisica – as a stand-in for the US – becomes clear when we consider its place in the original story. In the proposal presented to Tomoyuki Tanaka, Nakamura remembered,

> The tiny twins are spirited away by an entertainment producer from a certain country and brought to Japan, so the enormous Mothra travels the Pacific to

come rescue them, causing a panic in Tokyo. This was the stock-in-trade of the special effects team at [Toho], but the plot takes an intriguing turn as Mothra weaves a cocoon over the national parliament building. The JSDF is called into action to remove it. The three of us invoked the Treaty of Mutual Cooperation and Security between the United States and Japan as a plot device to justify Japan calling out the US Army for help, and then a group protesting the US-Japan security treaty forms around the parliament building. We leveraged actual news footage for part of this. Meanwhile, the Soviet Union attempts to use its veto rights at the United Nations in New York to block the US-Japan security alliance, leading to a tense series of debates. The film would interweave crosscuts of the Tokyo parliament building and the UN General Assembly in New York, with the crosscuts gradually getting more intense. Once it reaches a fever pitch, the cocoon bursts and the moth flies off the top of parliament in the final scene. At least, that plotline was my original proposal, but it was summarily rejected by Tanaka, who said something to the effect of, "That's the typical plotline you'd expect from a freelancer." (Nakamura in Nakamura, Fukunaga, & Hotta, 1994, 171–72)

As eventually written, *The Luminous Fairies and Mothra* is similar in basic structure to the finished film with its characters in place, Rolisica standing in for the US, and its ending in Rolisica's "New Wagon City". Also included were contextual details about the Shobijin, who are instead called the "Aelinas". A creation story is described which explains the Aelinas and Mothra as born of a pair of gods.

Importantly, both Nakamura's proposal and the published *Luminous Fairies* were openly informed by the mass demonstrations against renewal of the US–Japan Security Treaty (see Chapter One). *Luminous Fairies* features a similar treaty between Japan and Rolisica, facilitating the atomic heat cannon deployment later in the story.

However, Shinichi Sekizawa excised most of the overtly political material when penning the adapted screenplay. In the liner notes for *Mothra*'s LP drama record in 1984, Takeshi Narumi explains Sekizawa's approach:

> when Shinichi Sekizawa came to adapt the script, he entirely omitted the military treaty (which was an allusion to the [US–Japan] security pact). The attack on Rolisica's New Wagon City was relocated to Mount Kirishima in Kyushu and the

place where Mothra spins her cocoon was changed to Tokyo Tower which was then a well-known place having been completed in 1958.

Although Sekizawa diminished the overt commentary on the US–Japan Security Treaty, *Mothra* still speaks to Japan's post-war relationship with the US through Rolisica. The act of Rolisica – as a stand-in for the US – mobilising military hardware on Japanese soil to destroy Mothra emphasises these reflections. Given that continued American military presence in Japan had already brought specific examples of violence committed by US servicemen (as well as broader concerns over Japan's alignment with the US in the age of ICBMs), the failure of the heat cannons to stop Mothra suggests the destructive possibilities of American involvement – if not the redundancy of American military intervention for protective purposes.

On the other hand, at face value the film more immediately depicts improving relations between Japan and Rolisica. Earlier in the film, before Mothra arrives in Japan, Rolisica releases a statement saying it will protect the rights and property of its citizens, essentially an act of complicity in the Shobijin's exploitation. Eventually, Rolisica releases a secondary statement ordering Nelson to release the Shobijin in order to preserve Japanese–Rolisican relations. The subsequent lending of Rolisica's heat cannons to Japan and their hunt to stop Nelson are similarly presented as acts of improving international co-operation.

In the process, responsibility for Mothra's destruction and the harm done to the Shobijin is ascribed solely to Nelson, with Rolisica's wider culpability ultimately obscured by the end of the film. Of course, this is within the simplistic fantasy of Sekizawa's script, which had already removed much of the political specificity of *Luminous Fairies*. And *Mothra* is – by Sekizawa's own admission (see Chapter One) – a much lighter film than prior Toho monster entries anyway. Nevertheless, this lack of further interrogation *within* the film itself stresses the parallels with the Japan of 1961 as it moved further into post-war recovery and alignment with the United States; the contradictions, violence, and manoeuvring inherent to the two nations' wartime actions and post-war relationship becoming obscured beneath the narrative of stability and growth (Kohso, 2024).

Indeed, the improving relationship between Rolisica and Japan (complete with specific injustices going unaddressed) mirrors the latter's real-world post-war rehabilitation and assimilation into the Western capitalist mould via proximity to America – particularly when co-operation here is partly characterised via the lending of weaponry.

Themes of connection and co-operation are particularly pertinent at the film's climax. Despite Sekizawa's written ending at Kyushu, the actual finale takes place in New Kirk City in Rolisica – a stipulation from US distributor Columbia, who asked that the ending take place in an American-looking locale (Ryfle & Godziszewski, 2017, 177). This brings the film version closer to *Luminous Fairies*.

When the sun shines behind a crucifix atop a New Kirk church, Professor Chujo remembers the similarly cross-shaped Mothra symbol on Infant Island; the church bells also evoke the drums of Mothra's worshippers. After Chujo sees the cross, he shows Fukuda his sketch of the Mothra symbol, and Fukuda remarks that it must have religious significance on Infant Island. Thus, the film suggests that understanding one religious symbol can give way to understanding another; in turn this helps to resolve Mothra's rampage. An instance of cross-cultural recognition stirs resolution, chiming with Honda's broad hopes for international unity (see Chapter One). The New Kirk authorities agree to paint the Mothra symbol on an enormous scale on an airport runway far from the city. The plan works and ends Mothra's rampage. She reunites with the Shobijin and the trio return home.

That the Shobijin say goodbye with gratitude at the film's end – and not with resentment from Nelson's treatment – suggests that their trust has not been irreparably shattered. *Mothra* depicts trust as open to repair through redemptive action, affirmed by interpersonal, international, and cross-cultural connection. The film's characters all play a part in upsetting or repairing trust (both with the Shobijin and on the world stage), but their actions – villainous or heroic – are tangible. Comical moments like Zenichiro fighting with Nelson's cronies show him physically attempting to aid the Shobijin, dutifully trying to return the goodwill they have shown him. On an international level, world authorities actively look for Nelson in the third act; and effort is exerted to paint the Mothra symbol on the New Kirk runway.

Trust's betrayal and repair are therefore depicted in relatively simple terms in *Mothra*, characteristic of the broadly drawn heroes and villains Sekizawa writes. These ideas would become comparatively more complex in *Mothra vs. Godzilla*, with its narrative resolution drawn from promises rather than action.

Mothra vs. Godzilla begins with a massive typhoon. Mothra's egg washes ashore in Japan and is quickly purchased by greedy businessmen, Torahata (Kenji Sahara) and Kumayama (Yoshifumi Tajima) of Happy Enterprises. They plan to turn Mothra's egg into a profitable attraction and construction begins on a gigantic incubator. The Shobijin appear before the film's heroes: journalists Junko (Yuriko Hoshi) and Sakai (Akira Takarada), and scientist Professor Miura (Hiroshi Koizumi). The Shobijin beg them to return the egg to Infant Island, but the trio are unsuccessful in convincing the tycoons. To make matters worse, Godzilla was also washed ashore and soon begins a destructive march across Japan. Junko, Sakai, and Miura travel to Infant Island to try to convince the Shobijin to have Mothra fend off the marauding Godzilla.

Much as in *Mothra*, the Shobijin's trust is broken when Torahata and Kumayama refuse to return Mothra's egg, claiming it as their property. The businessmen also make an offer to *buy* the girls as well, immediately seeing more to exploit. Their offer reads as a satiric indictment of Japan's staggering economic growth in the 1960s, emphasised by an earlier conversation in which the heroes discuss Torahata's high-profile political connections. Torahata's absurd pursuits (commodifying a monster egg) reflect the similarly absurd rate and means of Japan's post-war recovery. His exaggerated greed encapsulates the era. In turn, as Yoshikuni Igarashi notes (in Tsutsui & Ito, 2006, 94), in *Mothra vs. Godzilla* there is no separate actor like Rolisica that primarily embodies capitalist enterprise and its exploitation, and which could therefore "[absolve] Japan of capitalist guilt". Instead, the greed here is entirely Japan's.

With the Shobijin's good faith spurned, their perception of the outside world – despite the heroes' support – is one of consumer greed. Consequently, the Shobijin and the people of Infant Island are unreceptive when Junko, Sakai, and Miura eventually ask for Mothra's help to defeat Godzilla. Here, trust becomes an overt part of the text; it is discussed by both the Infant Island Chief and the heroes. The Chief asserts that Infant Island's trust was repaid with treachery, heavily referring to the atomic tests wrought

Ghidorah, the Three-Headed Monster

against his people. Sakai speaks of the need to trust one another, and Junko mentions the good people who will die alongside the evil during Godzilla's rampage. She appeals to the Islanders' decency and humanity – virtues which have been denied to them.

In this scene, Junko, Sakai, and Miura arrive in a position of social debt, the Islanders scorned by Torahata and the greed of Japan he represents. They offer no real resolution and instead ask for Mothra's help, deepening the imbalance. Thus, *Mothra vs. Godzilla* explores the price of trust. The heroes are still saved because the Infant Islanders, the Shobijin, and Mothra put the people of Japan above the injustices done to them. Whereas the Shobijin are actively saved and helped by the characters in *Mothra*, they are forced to accept just a promise of Japan's decency in *Mothra vs. Godzilla*. Though the immediate crisis characterised by Godzilla is resolved by Mothra (and her offspring), trust between the heroes and Infant Island remains unresolved.

Shinichi Sekizawa hastily wrote three script drafts for *Mothra vs. Godzilla* between 31 December 1963 and 12 February 1964. Although specific details changed (in the first draft, Godzilla's washed-up body was set to be attacked by the military and doused with gasoline shortly before the creature awakens), the overall structure was largely consistent. Importantly, Mothra's egg washing ashore, its purchase by businessmen, and the denied request for its return were present in all versions. Kumayama was the only businessman originally, but an older gentleman, Manzo Torahata, was added in the second draft – eventually becoming his son, Jiro Torahata, in the final version (Suzuki in Kimura, 2022b, 82–84). These developments with Torahata allow the themes of *Mothra* to carry over into *Mothra vs. Godzilla*. After all, Torahata is functionally the same as Nelson, ruthlessly pursuing profit to the detriment of everyone else; he therefore continues *Mothra*'s criticisms of greed, though squarely Japan's this time around, as Igarashi notes. Moreover, just as the exploitation of the Shobijin stirred themes of goodwill, its betrayal, and an ensuing imbalance in *Mothra*, the similar profit-driven interest in Mothra's egg in *Mothra vs. Godzilla* returns us to that territory. However, *Mothra vs. Godzilla* mostly dispenses with the fairytale morality of *Mothra* in favour of a relatively more complex thematic delivery.

Now we come to *Ghidorah, the Three-Headed Monster* and the culmination of connection and co-operation. Trust takes a more abstract form here, extending to the monsters themselves. This is possible because *Ghidorah* sees Godzilla, Rodan, and Mothra become fully fledged characters, carrying themes in a much more active manner. It is therefore useful to explore how Sekizawa's script defined that development, and what it meant for the monsters' changing narrative function.

At the film's beginning, we learn that strange events are occurring all over the world: a heatwave in winter; an outbreak of Japanese encephalitis; and the icecaps melting. The arrival of King Ghidorah is simply the latest upset. In *Ghidorah*, imbalance goes beyond notions of a social contract between peoples, being rendered on an interplanetary scale. Ultimately, it is Godzilla, Rodan, and Mothra that reset the balance.

Before we discuss the monsters, let us first examine how these themes return in the human cast. Immediately, there is evidently an understanding and trust between the Shobijin and *Ghidorah*'s heroes – and Japan in a broader sense. The Shobijin appear on a live television programme, singing to Mothra for the audience's amazement. This is in stark contrast to the Shobijin's exploitative relationship with showbusiness in *Mothra*.

Although Detective Shindo, Naoko, and Professor Murai are not the same characters as in the previous film, they functionally serve the same purpose. In this way, the Shobijin's trust of the trio – though it may seem easily given – serves as an extension of that which was developed over the previous films. Furthermore, the tension that previously characterised the relationship between Japan and Infant Island is gone, replaced with what *appears* to be a somewhat better dynamic. The Shobijin appear as celebrities in Japan, and the Japanese government casually turns to them for help when King Ghidorah ravages the country.

The changing dynamics between the Shobijin and Japan parallel the monsters' development. *Ghidorah, the Three-Headed Monster* marks a decisively anthropomorphic edge to the Godzilla character. While *King Kong vs. Godzilla* brought comedy to the series, it is not until *Ghidorah* that the *character* of Godzilla (rather than the situations it is found in) displays an overtly comic side. Godzilla and Rodan laugh, cry out in pain, and clearly loathe the sight of one another. Shinichi Sekizawa was heavily involved in this characterisation. In a 1985 interview, Sekizawa explained his penchant for writing monster scenes in detail:

> I go into detail about this and that. I just like this whole aesthetic, so I delve right into it. You can imply a lot with how you depict it. To put the worst spin on it, I get carried away. I'd say run-of-the-mill screenwriters can probably put together a fight scene between humans, but most wouldn't be able to come up with such a detailed fight scene between monsters. But for me, it's a breeze. I know where to take the script and what to do with it. People often tell me that they can visualise a scene when they read my scripts. (Sekizawa in Endo, 1985a, 165)

Sekizawa's approach is evident in his description of *Ghidorah*'s climactic battle. In his final script draft, Sekizawa begins the scene as follows:

> King Ghidorah runs riot circling the foot of the mountain.
>
> Mothra approaches him.
>
> King Ghidorah glares at her as if saying, "What do you want, you little brat?"
>
> Incensed, he attacks with a gravity beam.
>
> Mothra is hit by rocks.
>
> But undaunted she vigorously spins silk.
>
> Ghidorah throws rocks at her again.
>
> Mothra presses forward.
>
> Like colliding with a *Yokozuna* [high-ranking sumo wrestler] during a bout, to move forward is to get pummeled.

In writing the specifics of the monster action, and especially in the voice he lends them ("What do you want, you little brat?"), Sekizawa gives definition to the monsters' anthropomorphic evolution. Indeed, Haruo Nakajima further confirmed this developing characterisation in Sekizawa's script, saying, "in this film, Godzilla showed his comical side, like talking to Rodan and Mothra... the script was made that way" (Nakajima, 2010, 145–46). While not every detail Sekizawa wrote made it to the screen, the broad beats of his monster brawls are there, embellished and expanded by Tsuburaya's direction and the performance of actors like Haruo Nakajima. For example, Nakajima himself was similarly integral to these character developments. Much of the actor's own body language wound up in Godzilla's physicality as the films continued, and especially in *Ghidorah*. Nakajima (2010, 146) recalled,

> In [*Ghidorah*], there is a scene where Godzilla sits like he was bored. That pose is my actual resting pose, when I take a rest without taking off the suit. Between the thighs, there was the battery to make Godzilla's mouth/eyeballs move, and it was in the perfect spot for me to sit on. I was so used to the suit, being hot inside did not feel like a big deal anymore, so I could even take a nap inside. It looked quite comical, so I think [Tsuburaya] decided to use that pose.

Ten years prior, Nakajima had turned to elephants to perfect Godzilla's gait, performing with a shuffling motion to emulate their movement. By 1964, Nakajima himself was informing Godzilla's body language. Thus, just as Sekizawa's specific writing gave shape to Godzilla's anthropomorphic characterisation, Nakajima and Tsuburaya physically realised it.

With Sekizawa, Nakajima, and others having made characters out of the monsters, they now serve new narrative roles. In Chapter One, we briefly discussed how the function of the monsters was changing by this point in the series. The consistent reappearance of the monsters means their existence alone is no longer the major source of narrative crisis. This is best exemplified when Mothra appears on television with the Shobijin. Neither Naoko nor her brother even register that Mothra – who recently saved Japan from Godzilla – is casually appearing on a variety programme. Instead, Detective Shindo reads a newspaper and Naoko talks about her work. There is a nonchalance towards the monsters; they still incite fear, but they are also an accepted part of this world.

In terms of what this means for the monsters' new narrative function, David Kalat observed in his 2007 DVD audio commentary that, "in the old paradigm, monsters threaten people, and people resolve it. In the new Japanese iteration, people threaten people and monsters resolve it".

In *Ghidorah*, the monsters (inadvertently or otherwise) resolve almost every story thread: it is King Ghidorah's gravity beams that destroy the Princess' assassins (this explicitly happens twice in the US version); Godzilla and Rodan thwart the assassins' plan to electrocute the Princess; and it is the combined strength of Mothra, Rodan, and Godzilla that forces King Ghidorah back into space. By placing the tools of narrative resolution in the hands of the monsters, the audience can view them with even greater depth.

Godzilla, Rodan, and Mothra stand victorious as King Ghidorah retreats into space. *Ghidorah, the Three-Headed Monster*. Producer: Tomoyuki Tanaka. Director: Ishiro Honda.

The monsters as characters with the ability to resolve crises is best exemplified in the "monster talk" scene, in which Mothra pleads with Godzilla and Rodan to set aside their differences to fight King Ghidorah. Again, Sekizawa gave form to the monsters' human-like behaviour here. For the scene's beginning, the final script draft reads:

Mothra moves towards Godzilla and chirps "Stop it!"

Godzilla and Rodan do not listen.

Mothra spits silk into Godzilla's face.

Godzilla tries to brush it off with his hands as if he were covered in cobwebs.

Rodan thinks it's incredibly funny and beats his wings.

Mothra's silk hits him in the face too.

Surprised, Rodan swings his neck wildly and angrily shouts at Mothra.

It is in this scene that trust reaches its abstract culmination. Godzilla and Rodan initially refuse to fight King Ghidorah, citing mankind's animosity toward them. Mothra argues that the Earth belongs to all and therefore must be defended. After Mothra heads off to fight on her own, Godzilla and Rodan eventually come to her aid. The monsters set aside their differences and fight together, captured in the climactic image of Godzilla, Rodan, and Mothra looking on as Ghidorah retreats. A new alliance is affirmed, and co-operation prevails between the monsters. Within this alliance, small moments mark their improved inter-monster relations, such as Godzilla actively allowing Mothra to bite onto its tail to pull her from harm's way – a change from when she aggressively bit Godzilla's tail in *Mothra vs. Godzilla*.

The audience, too, is part of this culmination. Just as the human characters begin to shift their perception of the monsters, so does the audience. Shindo berating Godzilla and Rodan for being "as stupid as human beings" opens them up to scrutiny usually reserved for human characters. In properly recognising the monsters as characters, and after seeing *them* trust one another in the fight against Ghidorah, the audience understands them better as well. In the process, the series finally catches up with several Godzilla manga stories that had already presented the monsters in comic, human-like fashion (see Chapter One).

Of course, this is not to suggest that a clear and defined separation between 'man' and 'monster' (either within the films or in terms of audience interaction) existed prior to *Ghidorah, the Three-Headed Monster*. As discussed in Chapter One, Godzilla offers an extension and reflection of Serizawa in the 1954 film; film critic Tadao Sato (DVD interview, 2011) has discussed audience identification with Godzilla as connected to the technology of its execution (i.e., monster costumes and the distinct physicality they produce); themes and suggestions of divinity in relation to Godzilla, Mothra, and Varan necessarily blur any ontological demarcations in conceptions of monster, nature, man, and the supernatural – and this has been emphasised by prominent *kaiju eiga* filmmakers like Noriaki Yuasa (BBC documentary, 1998); the personalisation and individuality afforded by the monsters' names also demands that we interact with them in a more focussed manner unlike that which is presumed for the often depersonalised *things*, *its*, and *thems* of contemporary American creature features. Rather, *Ghidorah* openly *stresses* the connections between man and monster in the overtly anthropomorphic characterisations of Godzilla, Rodan, and Mothra.

Though we will discuss the legacy of *Ghidorah* in Chapter Five, it should be noted that these shifts in character and their effect on audience perception laid an impactful foundation for future Godzilla films. Sekizawa's script for *Ghidorah* proved that the Godzilla character could be taken in new directions, and this alone may have secured Godzilla's cultural longevity as we know it. If *King Kong vs. Godzilla* showed that Godzilla could work in different genres, *Ghidorah* showed that the very character of Godzilla could decisively change.

Ghidorah, Godzilla, and Japan's New Image

In Chapter One, we explored how, among many ideas and evocations, Godzilla in the 1954 film embodies Japan's national character and processes of change. It is therefore significant that two months after the 1964 Tokyo Olympics – when images of a newly industrialised and economically powerful Japan were presented to the world – a friendlier Godzilla appeared in *Ghidorah, the Three-Headed Monster*. Of course, with mind to Jason Barr's (2016, 68–69) criticisms of overly broad and potentially reductive positionings of the monsters in these films as merely national signifiers, and cognisant of Aaron Gerow's (in Tsutsui & Ito, 2006, 63) astute observation that Godzilla's "semiotic wanderings" have always escaped singular enclosure, for the rest of this chapter we will return to Godzilla's capacity to reflect post-war Japan.

If we sustain the interpretation that Godzilla reflects facets of Japan itself, then the overt character transformation in *Ghidorah* expands our potential to explore issues of national identity. From atomic aggressor to humanised hero, Godzilla's evolution aligns with wider developments in the carefully constructed narrative of Japan's national character. The country had leapt from the ashes of war to an absurd position of economic growth. Its place in the international arena had gone from pariah to model of liberal democracy. Thus, 1964 was significant for Japan's national image, communicated through international and domestic spheres via the Tokyo Olympics.

The eighteenth Olympic Games of the modern era were opened on 10 October 1964 in Japan's National Stadium in Kasumigaoka, Tokyo. The site had been completed in 1958, a transformation of the Jingu Stadium which had, not long ago, played host to leaving rallies for college students conscripted for the war in 1943 (Igarashi, 2000, 144). The man in whose name they were sent, Emperor Hirohito, welcomed the world to a new Japan on the same site. In its very architecture, the Tokyo Olympics evoked the country's recent wartime past, with various former military sites converted into venues for the Games (Yoshimi, 2019). Similarly, the Olympic torch was lit by Yoshinori Sakai, chosen because he was born near Hiroshima on 6 August 1945. Of the many thousands of Japanese who watched the Olympics, Sakai's generation were born toward the war's end or in its aftermath and were coming of age in the post-war 1960s. The interactions of memory, war, modernity, and recovery were therefore all embodied in the 1964 Games.

The presentation of the Olympics both subconsciously and deliberately conjured wartime memories, a means to show a transformed Japan to the world by contrast. Daigoro Yasukawa, chair of the 1964 Olympics committee, said that the Games should highlight Japan "as a worthy member of the world family of nations" (McClain, 2001, 562). Japan's rapid economic recovery was on full display with Tokyo appearing as a modernised metropolis. Technological marvels like the Shinkansen bullet train, which went into public operation just prior to the Games, have become permanently associated with Japan to this day. As Sandra Wilson (2012, 160–61) observes, the Olympics enabled the Japanese government to "present new images of the nation… to show Japan in a positive light after the years of war, occupation, economic struggle and internal division".

As part of the Olympic preparations, residents near the stadium who had lived in temporary shelters and converted military barracks after the war were moved into the Kasumigaoka Apartments, with the first buildings erected to conceal the remaining wooden structures from public view (Mayumi & Sand, 2020, 438). In turn, this act of concealment necessarily highlights the artificiality and purpose of these new national images. For Yoshikuni Igarashi, the Olympics offered an easy answer to a difficult question of Japan's post-war identity. He states,

> The memories of destruction that haunted postwar Japan were admitted into

the Olympic arena insofar as they anchored a narrative of recovery from August 1945. It was the success of Japan that these memories ultimately invoked, and sufferings before 1945 were transformed into necessary conditions for the 1960s recovery. The juxtaposition of 1945 and 1964 in the Tokyo Olympic games encouraged spectators to make a short circuit from the destruction of 1945 to the reconstruction of 1964, leaving out the historical process of the nineteen years between. (2000, 145)

This image of Japan at the Tokyo Olympics was indeed a highly curated and carefully exported one. As detailed in Chapter One, the foundations of Japan's post-war course were laid not simply by the US, but in collaboration with agents integral to its imperial aggression. Systems of power that had enabled Japan's imperial atrocities remained intact, from the Imperial institution itself to the individual careers of politicians. Wonders of 1960s Japan, like the Shinkansen, similarly found their roots in the country's imperialism. Plans for the bullet train go back to the occupation of Manchuria, with the expansion of railways through conquered territories planned as a means of transporting supplies but also to encourage Japanese colonisation. Though the project was abandoned as wartime focus was drawn elsewhere, it was revived in the mid-1950s. Many of its engineers had not only worked on aircraft design during the war but actively took knowledge learned from the Zero fighter and applied it to the Shinkansen (Hood, 2006, 21–26; Harding, 2019, 273).

From war criminals like Nobusuke Kishi and the emerging dominance of the LDP, to powerful companies like Nissan and its investments in Manchukuo (McClain, 2001, 435–36; Harding, 2019, 268), the continuities from pre-war to post-war Japan challenge the familiar narrative of transformation suggested in the images of the Tokyo Olympics. Moreover, Hayato Ikeda's successor as prime minister was Eisaku Sato, Kishi's younger brother. And like his brother, Sato's tenure would also see the Japanese state violently exert itself against struggles and movements across Japan in the late 1960s and early 1970s (Kohso, 2024). In Sanrizuka, for example, residents and their allies (most of whom were farmers, a group largely left out of Japan's recovery as focus was drawn away from agrarian systems and toward industrialisation) fought the construction and maintenance of Narita International Airport – itself another symbol of post-war growth.

Indeed, the demonstrations against the US–Japan Security Treaty under Kishi, and the kind of anti-hegemonic politics of which they were a part, were similarly obscured by the narrative of change. After the LDP rushed its Treaty revisions through the Diet, effectively enforced by violent police action against protestors, William Marotti (2013, 3) notes how the party "sought a new legitimacy and a means to assuage and co-opt the defeated opposition by promoting a depoliticised everyday world of high growth and consumption and a dehistoricised national image in preparation for the Tokyo Olympics in 1964". The historical process to which these events belong was indeed left out of the Olympic image as Igarashi asserts.

However, images can be persuasive. The rapid rise in television communicated the image of change and expanded the nation's participation in the Olympics. As Wilson (2012, 161) notes, "only 50,000 foreign visitors came to Japan for the Olympics rather than the expected 130,000, but 65 million people around the country, or the equivalent of nearly 70% of the total population, are estimated to have watched the opening ceremony on television". As much as Japan was being presented to the world, these narratives were internally dispersed as well, a way to communicate the national self in a direct and highly visible manner after nearly two decades of "reform" and upheaval.

Cinema was similarly important for the communication of that image. As Inuhiko Yomota (2019, 110) notes, cinema became "the ultimate medium to restore the cultural pride that had been lost in the international arena". Several pictures in the post-war era aided perceptions of Japan, such as Akira Kurosawa's *Rashomon* (1950), which won the Golden Lion award at the 1951 Venice International Film Festival, and Kenji Mizoguchi's *Ugetsu* (1953), which won the Silver Lion award at the same festival in 1953. The curated export of Japanese films (and their critical acclaim) in the post-war years helped to signal recovery.

In terms of the Olympics, specifically, Kon Ichikawa's chronicle of the Games, *Tokyo Olympiad* (1965), carries much of the same symbolism as the event itself. The film begins with the Olympic torch being carried over several countries before eventually arriving in Japan. Upon its arrival, one of its first destinations is Hiroshima. The audience is introduced to the city with an aerial view of the "Atomic Bomb Dome", a common name for the Hiroshima Prefectural Industrial Promotion Hall (now the Hiroshima Peace Memorial). The building was close to the hypocentre of *Little Boy*'s detonation and was one of the few structures left standing. As the camera moves on, an enormous crowd is revealed standing near new buildings and architecture. A subsequent shot emphasises this stark contrast, first showing the Atomic Bomb Dome before pulling back to show an excited crowd welcoming the Olympic torch. The film, like the Olympics, deliberately invokes wartime memory to anchor the narrative of Japan's recovery by 1964.

Concurrently, films which, by way of their narrative content or international visibility, presented a positively transformed Japan sit on the other side of the cinema coin to pictures like *Giants and Toys* (1958, Yasuzo Masumura), *Blood is Dry* (1960, Yoshishige Yoshida), *Night and Fog in Japan* (1960, Nagisa Oshima), and many others. These films openly challenged the naked capitalism of Japan's recovery, depicting people's lives commodified and discarded within its narrative of growth. In particular, *Night and Fog in Japan* expresses frustration with the abandonment of radical politics as the forces of hegemony settled and reasserted themselves after the war, and more specifically in the aftermath of the 1960 Security Treaty protests.

Indeed, it is worth noting that Shochiku pulled *Night and Fog in Japan* (and therefore its release partner, *Blood is Dry*) from distribution within days of release, a decision that Yuko Shibata (2018, 5) places within the broader contexts of the depoliticised post-war everyday Marotti described earlier, stating that its limited exhibition was "an indirect result of the political upheaval caused by the Japanese government's attempt to solidify its alliance with the United States". The film's director, Nagisa Oshima, openly asserted the ideological nature of its withdrawal, arguing that "what killed *Night and Fog in Japan* is the same thing that killed Michiko Kanba…. What is it? It is everyone and everything that is displeased when the people try to effect reform from their side, to carve out new conditions for themselves. The enormous strength shown by the people in the fight against the security treaties terrifies and intimidates them" (Oshima in Michelson, 1992, 57).

Meanwhile, in the realm of Toho's own science-fiction–horror films, *Matango* envisions post-war wealth as an addictive fungus that mutates those who eat it while providing a state of ecstasy. The film unfolds on a mysterious island, and as each character submits to temptation and devours the deadly mushrooms, the message is clear: consume or die.

It is within this discourse of Japan's national identity, its changed image, the artificiality and purpose of that image, and how these discourses were reflected in cinema, that Godzilla's transformation in *Ghidorah, the Three-Headed Monster* finds additional meaning. In abstract fashion, the film serves as another communication of the new, curated, and positive Japanese position. Godzilla's heroism – though reluctantly shown – stands in stark contrast to the destruction the character embodied a decade earlier. The urgency of Godzilla's wartime association in the 1954 film is replaced by a friendlier, more human – and therefore more immediately identifiable – visage by 1964. Godzilla, like Japan, had shed its monstrous image.

Godzilla's association with the atomic bomb and the Second World War remains in public perception irrespective of any textual deviations. It is this facet of the character and series that, like the Tokyo Olympics and its deliberate invocation of wartime memory to anchor the narrative of change, draws focus to the settings in which Godzilla appears. By 1964, Godzilla, the wartime phantom, acting as protector and ally, calls attention to how far the national conversation had come. As Takayuki Tatsumi (in Fritzsche, 2021, 83) observes, there seems a contradiction in that "the destruction wrought by monsters who metaphorically stood in for the most powerful weapons of mass destruction in turn came to represent rapid cycles of reconstruction and recovery".

Yoshikuni Igarashi's analysis of *Mothra* and *Mothra vs. Godzilla* develops our understanding of the ways in which these monsters and their respective films came to embody – or, rather, were assimilated into – national narratives of recovery. Regarding *Mothra* and *Mothra vs. Godzilla*, Igarashi (in Tsutsui & Ito, 2006, 83–94) examines the ways in which Mothra and Infant Island embody specific tensions in their debut film, that Mothra's destructive rampage across Japan threads together capitalist greed, US–Japan military violence as reified by the Security Treaty, and a resurgent Japanese colonial view of South Pacific spaces in the 1960s as an exotified and imagined contrast to an industrial "centre" (consider Sekizawa's language regarding Mothra's origins in Chapter One, for example). He then contrasts this with how Mothra subsequently comes to *defend* Japan against Godzilla in *Mothra vs. Godzilla*.

In *Mothra*, tensions between the US and Japan are collapsed beneath the post-war narrative via the repaired relations between Japan and Rolisica. In *Mothra vs. Godzilla*, the *character* of Mothra is absorbed into this narrative as she fights – although reluctantly – to preserve Japan from Godzilla's destruction. In *Ghidorah*, these ideas are taken further when Naoko, her brother, and their mother watch as Mothra appears on a television programme. The tensions embodied by Mothra and the historical sites to which they are connected are also engulfed by the physical manifestations of post-war affluence – the private television set – with characters free to pick and choose when to tune in and consume Mothra's spectacle.

The "monster talk" scene is also worth examining in this regard. It gives form to Godzilla's new character image in presenting the monster with defined motivation and emotion, and the resultant battle with King Ghidorah completes the metamorphosis from antagonist to hero. That it is Mothra who convinces Godzilla and Rodan to unite – thus fulfilling their character transformations – is noteworthy. All three monsters are obviously of post-war origin, but Godzilla (and Rodan to a lesser extent) is much more specifically tied to the end of the Second World War. The dialogue and visuals of the 1954 film heavily evoke Hiroshima and Nagasaki, the Tokyo firebombings, and mass evacuations. *Mothra*, meanwhile, appearing in 1961 as Japan's economy boomed – technologically emphasised via the film's colour and widescreen photography – is clearly a later post-war creation. While the very recent and urgent political contexts that had informed *Mothra*'s production (i.e., the renewal of the US–Japan Security Treaty) are embedded within its story and presentation, they are handled in a comparatively less anxious manner.

The idea, therefore, of post-war Japan (via Mothra, in her colourful vibrance and themes of rebirth) engaging with its wartime past (evoked by Godzilla, and the associations of nuclear warfare and mass devastation inherent to the character) to unite for a secure future (in defeating the alien King Ghidorah) plays like an abstract reiteration of *Atragon*'s setup. Past and present meet in dialogue, and the post-war order ultimately prevails by rehabilitating the former.

King Ghidorah, specifically, also furthers Godzilla's transformation. Visually speaking, prior Toho monsters had all been giant versions of otherwise-real animals. Godzilla is an amalgam of several dinosaurs; Rodan resembles a pteranodon; Varan is essentially a giant lizard; Dogora is like a jellyfish; and Mothra is, of course, a gigantic moth. King Ghidorah possesses a comparatively unnatural form with three heads, two tails, and golden scales. Though its appearance finds its origin in various mythologies and fictional creatures, King Ghidorah's image befits the monster's extra-terrestrial origin. King Ghidorah's distinctly alien appearance separates it from Godzilla, Mothra, and Rodan, underlining that they are earthbound and thus closer to humanity by comparison. The "monster talk" scene again stresses this proximity in the monsters' highly anthropomorphic behaviour.

The first script draft for *Ghidorah* may have made these ideas more explicit. Indeed, the character Goro Aikawa, still under Venusian influence, says, "On Venus, there was nothing but science. But Earth has something that Venus did not have – Godzilla, Rodan, and Mothra" (Kaneda, 2018, 220). By highlighting Venus' lack of monster defenders, there is a suggestion that Earth is better for having them. While Godzilla and Rodan may have origins bound in mutation or ecological aberration, King Ghidorah's alien nature makes them appear much more natural and, insofar as they save the Earth by defeating Ghidorah, beneficial to the planet. As stated in Toho's 1983 Special Effects book, "King Ghidorah picks up all of the monsters' traditional roles regarding fear and violence, and all the Earth monsters turn into human-like characters" (Tanaka, 1983, 280). Additionally, in a 1984 interview, Ishiro Honda echoed these ideas, saying, "if the enemy comes from space, these creatures consider the Earth their habitat. For instance, animals have their territories and protect them, so I directed it with that in mind" (Honda in Kimura, 2023, 97).

As we explored in Chapter One, Vivian Sobchack's conception and description of the horror film can aid in structuring analysis, drawing out some of the more personal dimensions of the original *Godzilla* in the process. In turn, Sobchack's writing on the science-fiction film can similarly provide a framework to further clarify King Ghidorah's symbolic evocations and the ways in which the monster helps to further Godzilla's

Ghidorah, the Three-Headed Monster

character development. If the lens of horror allows for a richer reading of *Godzilla*, then a science-fiction structure can work similarly for *Ghidorah, the Three-Headed Monster*.

King Ghidorah's alien form provides specific avenues of analysis. *Ghidorah, the Three-Headed Monster*. Producer: Tomoyuki Tanaka. Director: Ishiro Honda.

Sobchack argues that the science-fiction film is about "society and its institutions in conflict with each other or some alien other" (2004, 29–30). As established, King Ghidorah's alien origin and appearance implicate Godzilla, Rodan, and Mothra as closer to humanity, emphasised by their humanlike behaviours. As they become *defenders* of Japan rather than its destroyers, they implicitly become *a part of* the society to which Sobchack refers; Mothra being called upon *by Japan* to mediate between Godzilla and Rodan reflects this development. Godzilla and Japan are *both* in conflict with the "alien other" that King Ghidorah represents. This is also visually reflected in the film's climax when the image of Godzilla, Rodan, and Mothra watching King Ghidorah retreat into space mirrors a similar shot of the human cast doing the same. Furthermore, we can look at the human characters as broad societal signifiers in their occupations, with Murai as a scientist, Shindo as a policeman, and Naoko as a journalist. The way in which these characters are seen to positively interact with one another (i.e., the sibling relationship of Naoko and Shindo, the hinted romance between Naoko and Murai, etc.), each playing a role in the narrative resolution, suggests a confidence in the systems of post-war Japan itself – if not the Western capitalist system of which the country was now a prominent example.

In particular, Shindo himself reflects the new, highly curated image of Japan. An international crisis unfolds on Japanese soil with the repeated attempts on Princess Salno's life, yet Shindo, a state enforcer, protects her at every turn. Her safe return home at the film's end works to depict Shindo as an effective policeman – an authority figure – and is therefore consistent with the narrative of Japan's newly secured position in the world.

Adding to the film's assimilation into and reflection of such narratives, as emphasised by the monsters' character transformations and King Ghidorah's otherworldliness, is what Sobchack (2004, 30–34) describes as a shift in focus of the science-fiction film away from responsibility for the monsters (as is often explored in the horror film) and toward the spectacle of the monsters' actions. As a space monster that arrives on Earth by accident, King Ghidorah's appearance is not the result of mankind's reckless use of science (as in *Godzilla*, *Rodan*, *Varan*, and *The H-Man*) or his greed (*Mothra*, *King Kong vs. Godzilla*, *Mothra vs. Godzilla*). The distinct lack of interaction between mankind and King Ghidorah arguably points toward a less anxious approach. This is not to suggest that King Ghidorah holds no symbolic, cautionary significance, but rather that the monster's appearance is not immediately bound up in introspective concerns over mankind's own behaviour – reflective of a comparatively more secure national image.

So, King Ghidorah as a non-specific, alien threat draws attention to Godzilla's human and earthbound characteristics, moving away from the introspection of the original *Godzilla* and toward a less emotionally complicated science-fiction spectacle. The film's conclusion sees King Ghidorah forced into space, defeated by the combined efforts of Godzilla, Rodan, and Mothra – who now sit comfortably alongside mankind both symbolically and textually. Thus, King Ghidorah is a national identity conflict made flesh. Godzilla, the former embodiment of wartime Japan, resolves the conflict and is therefore comfortably rehabilitated into the modern national body – coinciding with similar national narratives contained within the 1964 Tokyo Olympics.

King Ghidorah, Orochi, and Modern National Mythology

King Ghidorah as a personified national identity conflict also prompts a closer consideration of the sources that inspired the character. As discussed in Chapter Two, King Ghidorah's form took cues from Yamata-no-Orochi, the eight-headed serpent that battled Susano'o in the *Kojiki* and the *Nihon Shoki*. Indeed, that King Ghidorah has been called a "modern take" on Yamata-no-Orochi by Ishiro Honda (in Mirjahangir, 2022) asks that we consider other possible shared threads beyond just their visual similarities. When examining Orochi's place within the foundational narrative of Japan's Imperial family, for example, King Ghidorah as a kind of modern iteration complements the transformation of the Godzilla character.

The *Kojiki* and the *Nihon Shoki* detail the age of the gods and the birth of the Japanese islands, the former being the oldest extant work of Japanese literature; it was compiled in 712 and its name means "The Record of Ancient Matters" (Ono, 1962, 10). The two texts differ in their approach, but both begin with the story of how the gods appeared and their creation of the world. Regarding the *Kojiki*,

> The first or "upper" book follows the Gods of Heaven – the Amatsukami – as they come into existence and eventually send a pair of siblings, Izanagi and Izanami, to create the physical world. Izanagi and Izanami's children include the Sun Goddess Amaterasu and her estranged brother Susanowo. From this pair come a lineage of fertility gods, culminating in Ninigi, the Heavenly Grandson, who descends to the newly created world, where his descendants become the imperial clan. (Frydman, 2022, 27)

The Sun Goddess, Amaterasu, and her brother, Susano'o, are pertinent to our discussion of King Ghidorah. In the *Kojiki*, they are formed along with another sibling, Tsukuyomi, when Izanagi purifies himself in a river. From his left eye comes Amaterasu, Tsukuyomi from his right, and Susano'o from his nose. Amaterasu holds dominion over the heavens, Susano'o rules the ocean, and Tsukuyomi controls the night.

Susano'o strays from the sea because he misses his deceased mother, so Izanagi banishes him. In heaven, Susano'o seeks Amaterasu, whose trust he earns by creating three girls and five boys with her – the boys becoming her heirs. However, Susano'o rages with victory, running riot through heaven. He destroys its rice paddies and defecates in its sacred halls. He also causes the death of a weaving maiden when he drops a skinned horse into Amaterasu's weaving hall.

Ashamed, Amaterasu goes into hiding, only to emerge again when the gods lure her out by having a goddess perform in front of a mirror and jewel strand. Hearing laughter, Amaterasu emerges; the mirror and strand thus take on sacred power. These items become two of the Three Imperial Regalia (or the Three Sacred Treasures), handed down to her descendants in the Imperial family.

Meanwhile, the banished Susano'o goes to the Japanese islands. He finds a man and woman – local gods of earth – crying over their daughter. The couple originally had eight daughters, seven of whom have been devoured by Yamata-no-Orochi, a massive, eight-headed, eight-tailed serpent. Its body is said to fill eight valleys and cover eight mountains, and it has eyes like lanterns (Frydman, 2022, 183). Soon, the creature will return for their eighth daughter, Kushinada-hime. Susano'o offers to save her if he can take her as his wife.

To defeat Yamata-no-Orochi, eight platforms are constructed, each with a vat of sake. Orochi drinks from all of them and falls asleep. Susano'o then cuts off its heads and tails. His sword breaks when cutting into the eighth tail, but inside is an even mightier blade: the Kusanagi – this becomes the third item of the Three Imperial Regalia. Susano'o presents the sword to Amaterasu. She accepts and Susano'o remains in the mortal realm, where he settles with Kushinada-hime (Yasumaro, 2014, 18–27; Frydman, 2022, 36–40). In turn, the Kusanagi is passed down to Amaterasu's children who eventually conquer Japan, continuing the Imperial line. Thus, the act of defeating Orochi ultimately plays a pivotal role in affirming the imperial narrative.

The affirmation provided by the Three Imperial Regalia is still invoked today. Representations are present during the Imperial enthronement ceremony, most recently with the ascension of Emperor Naruhito in 2019. Moreover, amidst the economic revival of the 1950s, the washing machine, the fridge, and the black-and-white television set were called the "three sacred treasures". These eventually became the car, the air-conditioner, and the colour television by the late 1960s

(Yoshimi in Garon & Machlachlan, 2006, 76–77; Igarashi, 2000, 78–79). The symbolism of the Three Imperial Regalia, as suggestive of Japan's mythological foundations, was appropriated to legitimise the domestic comforts of post-war recovery – as indicative of an affluent nation.

Continuing that appropriation by broadly placing the story of the *Kojiki* in a modern, pop-cultural framework, *Ghidorah, the Three-Headed Monster* offers another perspective on Godzilla's character change. As established, the transformation of Godzilla's character reflects similar reintroductions of modern Japan on the world stage. One interpretation of the *Kojiki* views the slaying of Orochi and the offering of the Kusanagi to Amaterasu as Susano'o redeeming himself (Frydman, 2022, 39). Thus, if we take King Ghidorah's design heritage more literally, then defeating King Ghidorah, like Orochi, allows Godzilla to redeem itself for its prior destruction in a manner not unlike Susano'o. As Susano'o's victory helps to secure the Imperial line through the offering of the Kusanagi to Amaterasu, the victory of a heroic Godzilla – when interpreted as symbolic and reflective of Japan itself – suggests the narrative of post-war recovery. Indeed, from this point onwards in the original series, Godzilla is almost consistently a defender of Japan.

Of course, these parallels are admittedly broad in assertion and simplistic in analysis, especially when considering that interpretations, analyses, and depictions of the *Kojiki* and its stories are themselves highly varied throughout history and remain subject to political and ideological construction and dispersal – an immediate example being the institution of Shinto as Imperial Japan's state religion, with the *Kojiki*'s foundational myths employed to assert the superiority of the Japanese race, thus affirming both Japan's imperial ambitions and the *kokutai*. Moreover, there are also the differences between the stories as written in the *Kojiki* and the *Nihon Shoki* – and within the latter itself, in which multiple accounts of the same stories are referenced. However, as we have seen with the invocation of the Three Imperial Regalia to affirm post-war affluence (and vice-versa, with post-war affluence reifying national narratives), the act of flattening and appropriating these mythological foundations has been part of the post-war narrative construction, which – as we have also discussed in this chapter – is itself necessarily reductive and selective in its assembly and communication. If we understand the basic tenets of Susano'o's banishment and subsequent encounter with Orochi to be those of transgression, redemption, and continuation, these can, in essence, be mapped onto the exported post-war narrative, and therefore intersect with Godzilla's character developments in *Ghidorah*.

In turn, this emphasises the salient writing of Takashi Miura (2017) in his examination of religious themes and figures as they have been repeatedly reimagined and depicted in Japanese mass media historically, from the *kibyoshi* ("yellow covers", satirical illustrated fictions) of the Tokugawa era to their appearances in contemporary manga and anime. Miura notes, for example, how *kibyoshi* authors used reader familiarity with such figures (as well as their stories and the miracles associated with them) to place them in satiric or iconoclastic scenarios. Although he points out that the deities of the *Kojiki* and the *Nihon Shoki* did not appear as often in *kibyoshi* as other figures, they were still reinterpreted for comic use. One example by Koikawa Harumachi sees Susano'o's battle with Orochi reworked so that the former owes money to the latter (Miura, 2017, 236–38). While *Ghidorah, the Three-Headed Monster* is obviously not an exact retelling of Susano'o's battle with Orochi as it appears in the *Kojiki*, the reimagining of Orochi through King Ghidorah is both reminiscent of and in conversation with the ways in which deities and figures like Susano'o have been depicted and re-depicted, imagined and reimagined across mass media historically, from more direct adaptations like Toho's *The Three Treasures* and Toei Animation's *The Little Prince and the Eight-Headed Dragon* (1963, Yugo Serikawa) to films like *Ghidorah* which are several times removed.

Chapter Four: The US Release of *Ghidorah, the Three-Headed Monster*

Ghidorah, the Three-Headed Monster was released in the United States in late September 1965 by Continental, the distribution arm of the Walter Reade company. Like other Godzilla films prepared for US release, *Ghidorah* was significantly altered, necessitating an in-depth examination of the changes made.

Such an exploration requires a historical foundation. We will first discuss the American distribution landscape for both domestic science-fiction and horror pictures, as well as imported foreign films in the 1950s and 1960s. We shall then introduce the 1956 American release version of *Godzilla*, addressing its significance in exporting the film to the US and the precedent it set for future Japanese genre imports. We can then discuss *Ghidorah*'s US release as part of and influenced by trends in US film exhibition.

The American Genre Film Landscape

Until 1948, Hollywood's "Big Five" major studios (Warner Bros., Paramount, 20th Century Fox, RKO, and Metro-Goldwyn-Mayer) controlled their own production, distribution, and exhibition. Specifically, in terms of exhibition, they owned and operated their own theatre chains across America. Despite these "first-run" cinemas comprising just 15% of the total number of theatres in the US, they brought in almost 70% of box-office earnings. Once a film had played at these chains, it could then be shown at cinemas run by independent exhibitors. This involved the practice of "block booking": exhibitors would buy an entire season's worth of titles from a major studio to secure at least one hit by the time those pictures reached their theatres. However, a landmark anti-trust ruling had been working its way through the courts and would significantly alter how exhibition functioned (Heffernan, 2004, 2–3).

In May 1948, the US Supreme Court ruled that the majors' vertically integrated grip on exhibition restricted fair trade. Thus, the majors were divested of their theatre chains. Television was already eating away at moviegoing audiences, and the end of the Second World War heralded increased spending on consumer goods rather than cinema tickets. The reaction from the majors was to decrease the number of pictures made while investing in new technologies to entice audiences. Widescreen, new colour-film processes, stereophonic sound, and 3-D were all exploited to provide the kind of entertainment that television could not.

While the Paramount ruling (so named because Paramount was the largest of the Big Five) was intended to help the independent exhibitors, their situation was further complicated. Established theatre chains with links to the majors could partake in backdoor deals to book their pictures. As Samuel Z. Arkoff (Arkoff & Trubo, 1992, 28) explained,

> In fact, some of the theatre chain executives would congregate every Monday for their so-called "Boys Club" meetings, and illegally divide the available pictures among themselves; these circuits felt obligated to book most of the pictures from the majors, including weaker ones. With the independents, however, their negotiations were much tougher.

Adding to the woes of the independent exhibitors were the high costs involved in renovating their establishments to accommodate 3-D and other new technologies. Rental costs – the portion of a film's box-office gross paid to the distributor – were especially high for 3-D pictures. On 3 June 1953, an article was published in *Variety* which cited Theatre Owners of America president Alfred Starr. Starr argued that rental costs for 3-D pictures had been "determined not by quality or cost but by a preconceived and inflated notion of what the picture should gross without regard for public perception". Furthermore, he described a "gradual and insidious creeping movement by distributors, not necessarily limited to 3-D pictures, to exact exorbitant film rentals and to set up an entirely new pattern for dividing the box office dollar".

In the same issue, another article explained that many exhibitors were forgoing the installation of stereo sound systems altogether because of high costs. The article noted that "with stereophonic sound costing between $10,000 and $15,000 there appears to be no signs of a climb on the directional sound bandwagon. Attitude of small exhibs is that the chains can afford to spend stockholders' coin, but that the indie ops have to dig into their own pockets".

Ghidorah, the Three-Headed Monster

So, with fewer films being produced by the majors, increased rental costs to show them, and high prices for accompanying technologies, many independent exhibitors felt squeezed. This ultimately created the opportunity for Samuel Z. Arkoff and James H. Nicholson to start a company that would provide these theatres with the product they needed. American International Pictures (AIP) began as the American Releasing Corporation in 1955. Within their first year of operation, AIP hit upon a lucrative strategy: low-budget double-feature packages sold for the price of a single picture from the majors. Films shown on the lower half of a double bill generally earned a flat rate, whereas the top feature took a percentage. With AIP's packages occupying both halves, they netted a guaranteed profit. AIP also capitalised on teenage audiences with exploitation genre fare, accompanied by lurid advertising campaigns. Further helping independent exhibitors, several of AIP's combinations were released in the so-called "orphan" periods which saw fewer major releases and therefore a decreased number of theatre patrons. For example, AIP put out *Voodoo Woman* (Edward L. Cahn) and *The Undead* (Roger Corman) in March 1957, while *The Amazing Colossal Man* (Bert I. Gordon) and *Cat Girl* (Alfred Shaughnessy) were released in autumn that same year.

AIP rarely had big-name actors or high-budget productions with which to entice audiences. As Arkoff would later recall in the 2001 documentary, *It Conquered Hollywood! The Story of American International Pictures*, AIP had to sell exploitation, the idea that their pictures offered that which no other would or could. Other companies soon followed AIP's lead: Allied Artists put out a double bill of Roger Corman's *Attack of the Crab Monsters* and *Not of this Earth* in March 1957 to cater to the off-peak season (Heffernan, 2004, 98; Arkoff & Trubo, 1992, 86–87). So, exhibitors needed product, companies like AIP could supply it cheaply, and in order to compensate for lower production values, exploitation was indulged to entice audiences. And while practically every studio (both major and independent) produced science-fiction and horror product at some point in the 1950s, companies like AIP devoted a sizable portion of their output to the genre. Importantly, AIP identified and exploited the Paramount ruling's consequences in unique and highly influential ways.

CONSTELLATIONS

Godzilla Arrives in America

It was within this exhibition landscape that *Godzilla* made its widespread US debut in 1956. The Paramount ruling was influential in the film's journey to the States, primarily because of the opportunities it opened for producer, distributor, promoter, and showman Joseph E. Levine. Levine had entered the film business in the 1930s, founding his own company, Embassy, in 1938. He eventually owned several theatres in New England, and Levine practised the craft of exploitation releasing for a variety of film product. He had, for example, struck up a working relationship with Sam Arkoff and acted as New England distributor for AIP's early output.

In supplying films to product-starved exhibitors, Levine experimented with mass saturation bookings. This was a practice by which a film was released at multiple theatres simultaneously, accompanied by a major publicity campaign. In 1946, *Duel in the Sun* (King Vidor) was issued via the saturation method but proved unsuccessful at the box office. Levine noted that with an existing film – removing some of the financial risk – the saturation strategy could be lucrative. He acquired distribution rights for New England and re-released *Duel in the Sun* in 1954 via saturation booking; it played 250 screens in its first 21 days (McKenna, 2016, 22–34).

Godzilla offered Levine an opportunity to conduct the saturation booking method on a national scale. It should be clarified, however, that *Godzilla*'s US release was a collaborative effort, of which Levine was a significant part. The film had been bought from Toho in 1955 by Edmund Goldman of Manson International. It was then sold to Richard Kay and Harry Ross of Jewell Enterprises, who oversaw a complete re-edit of the picture. New scenes with American actor Raymond Burr were inserted, directed by Terry Morse. The film was also restructured to be told in flashback, beginning with the aftermath of Godzilla's second Tokyo rampage. In this new incarnation, Burr plays reporter Steve Martin, who investigates the disappearance of several fishing boats while on a layover to Japan.

Despite these changes, the film's mood and themes largely survived the editing process. Its flashback structure means that one of the first images presented to the audience is of a doctor scanning a child with a Geiger counter, only to shake their head in despair – a striking and evocative start to the film. Lines about hydrogen weapons resurrecting Godzilla also remain, and the nightmare visuals that constitute the monster's assault on Tokyo are enough to suggest the obvious parallels. Burr's performance is also one of sober, quiet horror.

However, some scenes were removed, including one in which commuters aboard a train discuss atomic tuna, evacuations, and escaping Nagasaki only for Godzilla to show up. In an interview, Richard Kay said that their idea was to make a movie they could sell, and that although there was no deliberate intention to downplay the film's messaging, politics did not interest them (Ryfle, 1998, 57–58). Regardless, the scene's removal makes this version less specific in its commentary than the Japanese original, and in preparation for American audiences its absence is distinct. For further reading, Steven Rawle's *Transnational Kaiju* (2022, 115–43) has examined the narrative and thematic effects of Burr's insertion, analysing an easing of the inherent American culpability in the subject matter.

For its US release, the film was titled *Godzilla, King of the Monsters!* (though some prints were shown bearing just *Godzilla*), which is the name we shall use hereafter (unless otherwise stated) to identify this version. Although Levine's exact point of entry into the operation is difficult to ascertain (McKenna, 2016, 37–38), what is known is that Embassy and Jewell formed a new company, Transworld, to distribute the picture.

To understand why the film (and others we shall discuss) was altered in such a way, it is worth briefly examining the history of exhibition for non-English-language foreign films in the United States during the 1950s. For the contextual purposes of our discussion, it must be understood that such pictures often saw limited opportunities for release. Most did not enter general release – the vast majority were shown in arthouse theatres – and few earned more than $200,000. There were sometimes exceptions, like Federico Fellini's *La Dolce Vita* (1960, US release 1961), which grossed $19.5 million. Nevertheless, by 1960, there were only 450 arthouse theatres across America, most of which were in New York or clustered in other metropolitan areas like Chicago, Los Angeles, or San Francisco.

The key distributors of foreign films were independent outfits operating out of New York City. They often obtained their pictures by putting up production money in exchange for US distribution or by visiting international film festivals and bidding on hits. Once in the States, a film would be subtitled for its arthouse release. If very successful, an English dub was produced which could play in more mainstream houses (what Balio [2010, 87] calls the "crossover" hit) as these theatres were generally averse to subtitled features. The dubbing process itself cost between $10,000 and $20,000, adding to the overall cost of distribution (Balio, 2010, 8–9, 85–88).

The history of Japanese film imports, specifically, adds to our exploration. Numerous high-profile Japanese pictures made their way to the States via the arthouse route. Festival hits like Akira Kurosawa's *Rashomon* (US release 1951) and Teinosuke Kinugasa's *Gate of Hell* (1953, US release 1954) impressed critics but mainstream, widespread exhibition proved elusive.

Considering the narrow environment for foreign, subtitled imports – most of which were pictures by renowned directors like Fellini, Kurosawa, or Jacques Tati – the opportunities for Japanese science-fiction films to play in their original format were slim. Even when Toho attempted to handle US distribution itself by opening its own cinemas in cities like Los Angeles (in 1960) and New York (in 1963), they predominantly played films from their most internationally recognised directors like Kurosawa and Hiroshi Inagaki – rarely their science-fiction pictures. Some special effects titles did play in Japanese with subtitles at select individual theatres that served local Japanese communities (Hawai'i was home to several such cinemas and even saw a release of the original version of *Godzilla* in Honolulu in 1955) but – as with many foreign films – they did not see *general* release in that form.

These localisation practices were, then, significant in enabling widespread mainstream exhibition for these films. At the same time, practices like the insertion of American actors also implicate the limits of general American audience engagement, and therefore the structures of American racism which informed those limits. As Richard Kay also said, "At that time, the American public wouldn't have gone for a movie with an all-Japanese cast" (Ryfle, 1998, 58).

Upon release, *Godzilla, King of the Monsters!* was very successful. Credit should be ascribed to Terry Turner, a master promoter for RKO who had worked with Levine in the early 1950s. Turner had overseen the publicity for both the 1952 re-release of *King Kong* and the 1953 release of *The Beast from 20,000 Fathoms* (McKenna, 2016, 38–39). That he would also handle the massive television and radio campaigns for *King of the Monsters!* directly connects *Godzilla* with its antecedents and inspirations.

On 4 April 1956, an entire page was taken in *Weekly Variety* to boast the film's impending release. "Mighty saturation" on television and radio was promised, with "color ads and a blasting newspaper campaign". Terry Turner's credentials with *Kong* and *Beast* were flaunted, with a quote from Turner praising the work of his colleague, Don Thompson: "I think 'Godzilla' tops any monster picture we have ever handled. Don's radio and TV spots will be the best he has ever made because this baby really breathes fire. Why gents, one short snort from this monster and 'poof' there goes another city". Turner's use of television was significant, turning "the ogre of Hollywood" into an asset. The success of *Kong*, *The Beast*, and *King of the Monsters!* played into his assertion that TV would eventually become the "golden goose of the film industry" (McKenna, 2016, 39).

Godzilla, King of the Monsters! opened at New York's Loew's State Theatre in late April 1956 before entering wider release across America throughout the summer. Levine, Turner, and company had a hit on their hands to satiate exhibitor demand. As noted in *Weekly Variety*'s 25 April review, the film "should generate [box office] excitement in houses geared to bally product and its offbeat nature is also worth attention of deluxers harassed by the current product shortage". The review would prove accurate. In Austin, Texas, nearly four months later, it was reported in the *Austin American-Statesman* that *King of the Monsters!* enjoyed packed showings at the Capitol Theatre. Commenting on the film's success, the article noted that "as it went into its second day, it appeared destined to give the Capitol a new box office record". Such success was mirrored all over the country, with *King of the Monsters!* playing on dozens of screens in multiple states.

The *Weekly Variety*'s review was also quite positive. Bar some criticism of the acting, the review praised its special effects, noting a "striking realism" to Godzilla's rampage. Although oft-cited, Bosley Crowther's scathing *New York Times* review was far from the standard critical reaction. Many critics throughout the United

States echoed *Variety*, criticising some elements while heaping praise elsewhere. For example, in July 1956, critic "B. E." for the *Spokane Chronicle* wrote that while there was "nothing particularly new about the story", the "excellent suspense and interesting shots of Tokyo and the Japanese coastal areas help to lift it well above the average film of this type".

The success of Levine's endeavour with *King of the Monsters!* can also be measured by how quickly Godzilla embedded itself within popular culture. On 25 July 1956, mere weeks after the film opened in California, the *Mirror News* of Los Angeles published a report on a local boxing match. Included in the copy was the line, "Making his second local start in two years, Ramon [Fuentes] had to come roaring on like Godzilla in the final two frames". The means and form of *Godzilla*'s American release allowed the monster to immediately embed itself in popular culture and consciousness.

Taking this further, Sayuri Guthrie-Shimizu's (in Tsutsui & Ito, 2006, 56–59) examination of *King of the Monsters!* situates the film's US success within the wider fabric of America's cultural intake, noting how localisation easily assimilated *Godzilla* into conversation with the many domestic science-fiction entries at the time which concerned similar fears of scientific possibility, from aforementioned titles like *The Beast from 20,000 Fathoms* and Corman's *Attack of the Crab Monsters* to *Tarantula* (1955, Jack Arnold) and *It Came from Beneath the Sea* (1955, Robert Gordon) – the latter of which features a giant octopus irradiated by Pacific hydrogen bomb tests, and which is said to have first destroyed several Japanese fishing boats. Guthrie-Shimizu's analysis, which identifies later US television syndication as instrumental in sustaining American interest in Godzilla films, is also emphasised by an article published in the *Charlotte News* in July 1956 called 'The Age of Anxiety Lives On – And On'. The piece described an American cultural appetite for destruction and horror in response to the kind of apocalyptic, nuclear anxieties that Susan Sontag detailed in her 1965 essay, *The Imagination of Disaster*. After mentioning television broadcasts of *Dracula* (1931, Todd Browning) and *Frankenstein* (1931, James Whale) as part of this phenomenon, the article specifically references the success of *Godzilla, King of the Monsters!* as further evidence, highlighting the salience with which Guthrie-Shimizu situates *Godzilla*'s localisation within the American cultural landscape.

Stateside Success in a Changing Release Landscape

Godzilla, King of the Monsters! ensured that further Toho monster films could enter the US market. *Rodan* was prepared for stateside release in 1957 by the King Brothers, distributed in the US and Canada via Distributors Corporation of America (DCA); RKO handled overseas distribution. Like *Godzilla*, the film was re-edited for its US release, though in a different manner. While *Rodan* did not see an American actor inserted into the story, several changes were made. The sequence of events was rearranged; pieces of Akira Ifukube's music were removed and replaced with American cues; alternate special effects shots were included, and sound effects were changed during the two Rodans' attack on Fukuoka (which was changed to Sasebo via the English dubbing). The dubbing cast included Keye Luke and George Takei.

A newspaper advertisement for *Rodan*'s New York release with its area co-feature, *Battle Hell*. Originally printed in the *Daily News*, New York, 15 March 1958.

When *Daily Variety* reported on the King Brothers' distribution deal with DCA on 20 September 1957, they highlighted the significance of *Rodan* (and therefore its peers) playing in mainstream houses: "Film, carrying a total investment of $700,000, will go into general release in November, instead of playing art house circuit, generally the case with [Japanese] imports". Indeed, *Rodan* – like *King of the Monsters!* – enjoyed a massive release in the US. On 19 March 1958, it was reported in *Weekly Variety* that *Rodan* had been booked into 79 theatres in the New York metropolitan area, running an average of four days to a week. From this area alone, DCA earned between $450,000 and $500,000, having spent $80,000 on TV advertising. The article also quoted DCA sales chief Irving Wormser, who said that *Rodan* (and its area co-feature, *Battle Hell* [1957, Michael Anderson]) had performed better than "any recent science fiction picture" and that its returns "equalled or bettered" those of recent blockbusters. *Rodan*'s New York success was echoed in the 14 April 1958 edition of the *Film Bulletin*, which said the use of TV was "also credited to the film's turn-the-crowds-away performances in Kansas City, Chicago, Minneapolis, and Seattle".

Rodan received critical praise to match its financial success, with critics actively addressing the efforts of key technicians in their reviews. A review published in the *Galveston Daily News* of Texas in November 1957 offered particular praise for the camera work: "Like a conductor wielding a baton, director of photography Isamu Ashida indeed skilfully handles a veritable symphony of color". The special effects also received commendation, with the author singling out Eiji Tsuburaya for compliment:

> Of equal stature with the striking use of color is the memorable work of Eiji Tsuburaya, deemed the best director in the "special photographic effects" field in Japan, and the creator of the unusual photography of the chilling "Godzilla" – a feat which many feel he has surpassed with the incredible supermonster, Rodan.

In December 1957, Helen Bower (25) delivered a perceptive review for the *Detroit Free Press*. After noting the visibility of the Japanese film industry since the war's end via critical successes like *Seven Samurai* (1954, Akira Kurosawa), Bower read into *Rodan*:

> As the country which felt the impact of the first atomic bomb, Japan may understandably be more acutely conscious than other countries of the perils of the atomic age. This awareness is implicit in the screenplay's thesis that effects of atomic and hydrogen blasts may have penetrated to the depths of the earth with fantastic result.

Bower ends by noting how recently it was that Japan existed under occupation, and thus her review situates *Rodan* within relevant industrial, social, and political contexts.

Rodan proved that the success of *King of the Monsters!* was no anomaly. *The Mysterians* was quickly picked up by Edmund Goldman and Paul Schreibman in January 1958 – to be handled in association with Joseph Levine. From there, Levine took the film to RKO, but it was MGM (another of the original Big Five) that bought distribution rights in February 1959; Terry Turner was also hired to promote the film.

Toho took notice of these successes. It was reported in *Weekly Variety* in September 1958 that Toho was asking $150,000 for a potential US release of *The H-Man*. This came to pass by January 1959 when Columbia (formerly one of Hollywood's "Little Three", along with Universal and United Artists) picked up worldwide distribution rights. Columbia went all in on exploitation with a travelling trailer. As reported in the *Film Bulletin* on 22 June 1959, Columbia's trailer visited 36 cities across eight states. Spectators were invited inside to experience "a three-dimensional, animated 'H-Man', bubbling atomic pools, dripping phosphorescent water, ultra-violet lighting and eerie sound effects".

The release of these films by Columbia and MGM coincided with a growing Hollywood interest in overseas pictures in the late 1950s. Columbia led the charge in 1957, distributing foreign pictures via Kingsley International and therefore bypassing the Motion Picture Association of America (MPAA) rule that member studios could not distribute films without a Production Code seal – which foreign pictures often lacked. Columbia also signed Jean-Luc Godard in 1963 to a multi-picture deal with budgets between $100,000 and $120,000, releasing them through Royal Films (formed in 1962 after Edward Kingsley died). United Artists distributed and sometimes financed films from Europe in the mid-1960s, while Universal began involving itself with a selection of British films and studios from the end of the 1950s through the 1960s (Balio, 2010, 229–39; Kinsey, 2002, 144–46).

Increased involvement in foreign films from the larger Hollywood studios may have influenced *Ghidorah*'s US release. Its distributor, Continental, was one of six key independent companies importing foreign films in the 1950s, operating out of New York City. It worked as an exhibitors' co-operative, putting up money to finance films in exchange for first-run exhibition rights (Balio, 2010, 83–85). Meanwhile, its parent organisation, the Walter Reade company, owned and operated several first-run arthouse theatres in Manhattan. Via Continental, Walter Reade's arthouse releases included Jacques Tati's *Mon Uncle* (1958) and Kurosawa's *High and Low* (1963) among many others.

The Big Five's entrance to the art-film market heralded the construction of further arthouse theatres in Manhattan. The majors intended to use these arthouse screenings to build attention around a film before a potential general release. However, there was not enough product to actually show, and domestic films were often booked into these theatres. Combined with the rising overhead costs of advertising, independent distributors were squeezed (Balio, 2010, 241–47). Continental was one of the only independent arthouse distributors to survive into the 1960s, though its financial situation was grim.

Company head Walter Reade jr. recognised that staying solely in the art-film market was certain doom. As he said in *Daily Variety* in September 1965, "you can't take good reviews and awards to the bank". Continental therefore began distributing more mainstream films for general release. Its eight films for 1965's final quarter included a fairly even variety of arthouse and mainstream pictures. *Ghidorah* was one of the latter.

Assembling *Ghidrah*

Ghidorah was released in the US as *Ghidrah, the Three-Headed Monster*. The Walter Reade version constitutes an extensive re-edit of the original film, with the sequence of events rearranged, some scenes cut altogether, and others shortened. Many of these alterations streamline parts of the story while others are less accomplished. For the remainder of this chapter, we shall refer to the film as *Ghidrah* to specify its localisation.

A significant edit occurs early in the film. In the Japanese version, the sequence runs as follows: the UFO club spots the meteorite shower and then we cut to the police station to see Shindo receiving his orders from the chief. Next, Salno is possessed by the Venusian voice aboard her plane and then King Ghidorah's meteorite lands. In the US version, the meteorite landing is brought forward to take place immediately after the UFO club spots the meteor shower. While the Japanese sequence plays to the Venusians' clairvoyance, the American sequence directly ties Ghidorah's arrival to the shower.

Another shift is King Ghidorah's birth itself. In the Japanese version, Salno undergoes treatment at Dr. Tsukamoto's laboratory before waking to reveal King Ghidorah's presence on Earth; Godzilla and Rodan brawl near Mount Fuji; Professor Murai and his fellow scientists watch as Ghidorah's meteorite activates; finally, a warning is broadcast before Ghidorah flies over Matsumoto.

In the US version, the sequence runs differently: King Ghidorah emerges from the meteorite first. Salno then wakes at the laboratory and speaks about the monster; Dr. Tsukamoto says it would be a bad situation if King Ghidorah came to Earth, to which she replies, "It's worse, because he's arrived". We instantly cut to the warning broadcast before Ghidorah appears over Matsumoto. We return to Tsukamoto's laboratory as Salno lies down to rest, and then we finally see Rodan and Godzilla fighting.

This is one of the strongest edits in the localisation. In the Japanese version, Salno's conversation continues after she reveals King Ghidorah's presence on Earth, somewhat diminishing the shock of that information. By contrast, the US version appears more impactful because although the audience has – in this sequence of events – already seen the monster, Salno's revelation is punctuated by a hard cut and the thundering piano keys of Akira Ifukube's score.

A weaker alteration occurs when Godzilla emerges at Yokohama. In the Japanese version, we see a burning ship as people look out at the water. Godzilla is then revealed, half-submerged. The people scatter and Godzilla fully appears on land. In the US edit, we see fleeing crowds in the city (shown later in the Japanese version) before cutting to Godzilla on land. When we next see Godzilla, the monster is back in the water, half-submerged. This renders a continuity error.

Nevertheless, the Yokohama landing sequence also demonstrates how the US cut repurposes shots in interesting ways. In the Japanese version of the scene, Rodan appears in the sky after Godzilla has properly come ashore. In the US edit, some of these Rodan shots are removed and are instead used earlier when Godzilla first appears in the film, rising from the ocean to blast a ship with its atomic breath. The US edit inserts the Rodan flight shots just before Godzilla emerges from the waves. It has the effect of suggesting that Godzilla surfaced in pursuit of Rodan. Moreover, an inserted close-up of Godzilla roaring (also originally from the later Yokohama scene) makes it seem as though incinerating the ship is akin to an angry reaction, which builds anticipation for the two monsters' eventual confrontation at Mount Fuji.

Elsewhere, another example of repurposing shots occurs when Malmess is killed by an avalanche during the climax. In the Japanese version, we assume the avalanche is triggered by the monsters, but it is not explicit; we hear but do not see Ghidorah's gravity beams. The US version inserts earlier shots of Ghidorah to make it unambiguous that the monster causes the landslide.

The climax also demonstrates how added stock cues from American composers affected the film's atmosphere. In the Japanese version, Malmess' last-ditch attempt to assassinate Salno plays without music. In the US version, a stock track by Trevor Duncan (titled "Slow Burn") is inserted and raises the tension. Another Duncan track, "Smoke", is added early in the film when Professor Murai and his colleagues hike to King Ghidorah's meteorite.

Other added tracks were composed by Paul Sawtell, the melodies of which can be heard in earlier genre titles like *The Animal World* (1956, Irwin Allen) and *The Black Scorpion* (1957, Edward Ludwig). Music by Anthony Bridges was also included. His track "The Chase" replaces Ifukube's cue when Rodan emerges from Mount Aso; it was originally released in 1963 as part of *Major Production Music*, an album of stock cues for use in film, radio, and television.

Joseph Bellucci, of Bellucci Productions, handled the English dubbing. Originally of Chicago radio and TV, Bellucci had worked as a dubbing director since at least the early 1950s (Tubbs, 1951, 73). He had supervised dubbing for films by Fellini and Vittorio De Sica (Robinson in Homenick, 2018b), and had directed Rhoda Williams when she voiced Brigitte Bardot for *The Night Heaven Fell* (1958, Roger Vadim), which was released in the US by Columbia via Kingsley International (Skolsky, 1958, 5). *Ghidrah* was not his first Toho picture, either; he had already directed the dub for

Battle in Outer Space (1959, Ishiro Honda). A story alteration carried by the dub is that Salno says she comes from Mars instead of Venus.

Ghidrah's alterations are some of the most interesting of all the localisations discussed in this chapter. Many of them are almost imperceptible, found in rearranging or repurposing single shots within a given scene. While some of the changes are flawed, the more significant alterations play to the film's strengths, tightening the pace and highlighting the most pertinent information for the audience.

Ghidrah Conquers America

The Walter Reade company (then called Walter Reade-Sterling after merging with Sterling Television in 1961) distributed *Ghidrah* in the US via Continental in September 1965. In the *Motion Picture Exhibitor*, *Ghidrah* was listed as one of Continental's key releases for the autumn 1965 period. A two-page spread was similarly taken in *Daily Variety* on 23 September to advertise the company's "Golden Quarter" releases, which included *Ghidrah*.

Walter Reade-Sterling's recognition of *Ghidrah*'s wide appeal is evident in Continental's showman's manual. A full-colour children's King Ghidorah mask was designed which could be ordered and made available at theatres. Various newspaper ads from across the country reveal that select cinemas did indeed offer the mask to their patrons. Continental also suggested that retailers offer the mask in conjunction with their own sales; children's television hosts were similarly encouraged to gift the mask to their guests. As with *King of the Monsters!* and *Rodan*, several TV and radio spots were prepared.

The Elvis Presley vehicle *Harum Scarum* (1965, Gene Nelson) and the James Bond spoof *Agent 8¾* (1964, Ralph Thomas) have often been cited as co-features for *Ghidrah* in the US (Ryfle, 1998, 117; Kalat, 2010, 76). However, it should be clarified that *Ghidrah* never had an official co-feature release partner. A year prior, *Mothra vs. Godzilla* had been distributed in America via AIP (as *Godzilla vs. The Thing*) in a package with *Voyage to the End of the Universe* (a US localisation of Jindrik Polák's 1963 *Ikarie XB-1*) but *Ghidrah* was, by contrast, released with several dozen titles across different territories and individual theatres during its theatrical circulation.

A newspaper advertisement for a showing of *Ghidrah, the Three-Headed Monster* in Wichita Falls, Texas, mentioning Continental's mask tie-in. Originally printed in the *Wichita Falls Times*, Texas, 28 September 1965.

Ghidrah's pairing with *Harum Scarum* did not properly begin until December 1965. For example, the pair played a saturation release together in the New York metropolitan area starting 15 December. That same month, *Ghidrah* also played a saturation run for a week in Philadelphia, where it was paired with *Sands of the Kalahari* (1965, Cy Endfield), a film executively produced by Joseph Levine. Also in December 1965, *Ghidrah* was shown with *The Blob* (1958, Irvin S. Yeaworth) at multiple theatres in and around the San Francisco Bay Area. *Agent 8¾* and *Ghidrah* were briefly paired at the Crown theatre in San Francisco in late December 1965, and were then shown together at a handful of cinemas throughout 1966. For example, in January 1966, they were paired in Chester, Pennsylvania at the Congress theatre. They were paired again in April at cinemas in Massachusetts, Georgia, and Hawai'i. The films also received a saturation run together across multiple theatres in Pittsburgh in May 1966.

Beyond these noteworthy releases, there were various pairings at individual theatres. Newspaper listings reveal such examples as *Horror Castle* (1963, Antonio Margheriti), which was shown with *Ghidrah* for almost two weeks at the Palms theatre in Detroit, Michigan starting in late October 1965. *Reptilicus* was shown with *Ghidrah* at two theatres in Fresno, California for a few days in early December 1965. *The Time Travelers* (1964, Ib Melchior) was paired with *Ghidrah* for a week at Green Acres drive-in theatre in Newport News, Virginia in January 1966. *Planet of the Vampires* (1965, Mario Bava) and *Die, Monster, Die!* (1965, Daniel Haller) formed a triple bill with *Ghidrah* in late April 1966 at the Gala and Blue Sky drive-in theatres in Akron and Wadsworth, Ohio, respectively.

Most of these examples would have been assembled by individual theatre and drive-in owners. In any case, they make up a very narrow slice of the variety of films shown with *Ghidrah* during its release.

When Continental released George A. Romero's *Night of the Living Dead* in 1968, *Ghidrah, the Three-Headed Monster* sometimes played as its second (or third) co-feature. This newspaper advertisement shows such an engagement, along with *Dr. Who and the Daleks* (1965, Gordon Flemyng). Originally printed in the *Reno Gazette-Journal*, Nevada, 31 October 1968.

Critical reaction to *Ghidrah* was mostly positive, with many critics praising the effects and direction. On 5 October 1965, "Robe" reviewed the film in *Daily Variety*, offering an illuminating comment pertinent to our look at Godzilla's character in the last chapter. Robe noted Tsuburaya's ability to give the monsters human qualities, "with Godzilla the walkaway champ in personality but Mothra the most sympathetic". Honda's input was praised, too: "When the viewer finds himself cheering on the trio of unlikely allies, it's a tribute to Honda's ability to capture an audience".

In December 1965, Ann Guarino (96) of the *Daily News*, New York, praised *Ghidrah*'s execution: "The story is treated with scientific overtones and imaginative special effects against beautifully photographed settings". The *Colorado Springs Gazette-Telegraph* also highlighted Tsuburaya's work on 22 January 1966: "Master special effects creator, Eiji Tsuburaya, is again responsible for the action which calls for the realistic destruction of ships at sea, the city of Yokohama and villages unfortunate enough to be in the path of the havoc-bent monsters".

Louis Cook (1965, 23) of the *Detroit Free Press* downplayed the film as "cheerful baloney", but nonetheless offered an amusing comment: "You really need a score card to keep your monsters straight these days, although there is a large and avid audience of specialists who keep track of The Blob as carefully as if it were Debbie Reynolds". Other critics were far more dismissive. Louis R. Cedrone jr. (1965, 18) wrote in Baltimore's *Evening Sun* that *Ghidrah* was "a terribly silly, badly done thing", adding that "The acting is bad, the dubbing more so and the special effects range from amateurish to exceptionally good".

Nevertheless, *Ghidrah* did good business. As early as 3 November 1965, *Weekly Variety* reported Continental's bettered outlook. The piece singled out *Ghidrah*'s Boston run, from which it had earned $200,000 in its first five days. *Ghidrah* was once again highlighted as a winner for Continental a few weeks later, on 24 November, with *Weekly Variety* noting that,

> According to [Walter Reade jr.], as a result of such pix [*sic*] as "Ghidrah, the Three-Headed Monster" and "Agent 8¾", the final quarter of this, Continental's 13th year, will be the biggest in the history of the company, both in dollar gross and in total number of theatres serviced. He expects the rentals on "Ghidrah" to be in excess of $1,300,000.

In a January 1966 interview, Walter Reade Jr. said that Continental's losses in 1964 were $1,200,000 (Wolf, 1966, 17), making his projections of $1,300,000 in rentals for *Ghidrah* especially significant. In that same piece, Reade affirmed the move toward more mainstream pictures: "In the market today it is impossible to have a commitment to only one genre of filmmaking". *Ghidrah*, along with other films, was proving his assertion in its critical and financial success.

Ghidrah, the Three-Headed Monster would be the last Godzilla film released theatrically in the US until 1969. Henry G. Saperstein, who had co-financed 1965's *Invasion of Astro-Monster* via United Productions of America (UPA), had sought a US theatrical release (under the name *Invasion of the Astro Monsters*) but distribution was not secured until 1970 through Maron Films, by which time it had been rechristened – first as *Invasion of the Astros* in a limited capacity at US military bases, and then as *Monster Zero* for its wider release. Meanwhile, *Ebirah, Horror of the Deep* and *Son of Godzilla* (1967, Jun Fukuda) were released directly to television through Walter Reade-Sterling in 1968 and 1969, respectively. It was *Destroy All Monsters* (1968, Ishiro Honda) that saw Godzilla return to US cinema screens, distributed by AIP in the summer of 1969.

Toho, Hammer, and the Wide Reach of American Film Interests

Henry G. Saperstein's involvement with *Invasion of Astro-Monster* is significant. Much as the bigger Hollywood studios had started involving themselves with various overseas productions and filmmakers by the 1960s, so too did Toho engage in direct co-production with various American outfits for several of its special effects films. This clarifies that, in many cases, the processes of localisation and/or alteration were not simply enacted upon import, but were instead incorporated during the scripting, financing, and casting of these films. This Hollywood influence also intersected with trends in the Japanese film industry.

In this next section, we will look at direct American involvement and influence in the production of Toho's monster films and those of other Japanese studios. We shall also compare US presence in Toho's filmography with American involvement in the output of other non-US producers of horror and science fiction – in this example, Britain's Hammer Films – to provide a wider perspective on Hollywood hegemony in overseas filmmaking and specifically in the making of genre product.

As detailed earlier in this chapter, Toho noticed the success enjoyed by *Rodan* in the States and actively began looking for a US distributor for *The H-Man*. Moreover, although *Giant Monster Varan* eventually received a standard Japanese theatrical release, it was originally made for episodic broadcast on US television (Jampel, 1959, 46). Similarly, Columbia's involvement in *Mothra* determined the location of the film's climax (see Chapter Three). Hollywood presence in Toho's special effects films – whether in the search for US distribution arrangements, production plans with the US market in mind, or American studio influence over narrative content via financial backing – was well established by the time Henry G. Saperstein began working with the studio. In turn, Saperstein would provide financing for several Toho science-fiction films in the 1960s, offering input to make them more marketable abroad.

Japanese studios looked to foreign release opportunities as the industry decline of the 1960s set in. Three major studios (Daiei, Nikkatsu, and Shochiku) took advantage of the Film Export Promotion Association, an organisation established under the control of the Ministry of International Trade and Industry after years of studio lobbying for government financing. Operating between 1966 and 1971, it subsidised production of export-appropriate films through government loans. As Takeshi Tanikawa (in Bernardi & Ogawa, 2020, 114) explains, "the studios were expected to make a maximum effort to export the subsidized films". With the financial success of Japan's monster films abroad, several titles received government funding, such as Nikkatsu's *Giant Monster Gappa* (1967, Haruyasu Noguchi) and Shochiku's *Giant Space Monster Guilala* (1967, Kazui Nihonmatsu). It should be mentioned, however, that Toho pressed ahead without this support.

As Tanikawa notes, a recurring characteristic of several export-appropriate monster films was their inclusion of a foreign actor. Gamera series director Noriaki Yuasa confirmed this trend, recalling that including a foreign character became standard for the Gamera series after it first received export funding (Tanikawa in Bernardi

Ghidorah, the Three-Headed Monster

& Ogawa, 2020, 118). Thus, one of the most overt signifiers of localisation – the insertion of American actors – was being incorporated from inception in some cases. Toho did the same when casting Nick Adams in *Frankenstein vs. Baragon* (1965, Ishiro Honda) and *Invasion of Astro-Monster*, as well as Russ Tamblyn in *War of the Gargantuas* – all co-financed by Saperstein and/or UPA.

Several US localisations have also found exhibition and use within Japan itself. Notably, *King of the Monsters!* was released in Japan in 1957 as *Monster King Godzilla*, cropped to widescreen format. Furthermore, in some cases Toho has adopted US release cuts for their own English-language export versions. Like many studios, Toho often commissioned the production of English dubs for several of its titles. These English-dubbed export/international versions (complete with their own English-language title cards and credit sequences) could then be offered to Anglosphere distributors or provided as the basis for dubbing into other languages in various markets. While US distributors in the 1960s usually opted for their own dubbing (via outfits like Titra Studios), Toho's export dubs saw more use in the 1970s as the basis for several American Godzilla localisations.

Regarding *Ghidrah*, specifically, Toho actually used the Walter Reade version of the film to construct an English-language export trailer – likely in the early 1970s – featuring both its particular dubbed vocal performances and its unique title card. Toho has also provided the Walter Reade *Ghidrah* for repertory screenings in the US, such as in 2004 at Grauman's Egyptian Theater in Los Angeles for a fiftieth-anniversary Godzilla festival. Similarly, while evidence suggests that an export version of *Invasion of Astro-Monster* may have been prepared, Toho eventually adopted the UPA dub (and a corresponding early title sequence for the UPA version bearing the name *Invasion of the Astro-Monsters*) to construct an international edition. This international version of the film was also shown at the 2004 Godzilla festival and has been released on VHS in several markets, including Britain.

Speaking of Britain, the history of Hammer Films demonstrates the far-reaching processes of localisation, co-production, and American influence in non-US genre production. Though there are obviously differences between Hammer, Toho, and their respective filmographies (discussed later), the following comparison intends to highlight that both were prolific producers of high-profile genre fare operating outside of but regularly interacting with Hollywood – if not America in a broad sense. Comparison is also affirmed by Henry G. Saperstein. Prior to working with Toho, Saperstein's salesmen approached him with a need for science-fiction product, and so he asked the Academy of Motion Picture Arts and Sciences about who made the best monster films. "The reply was Hammer Films in England and Toho in Japan" (Saperstein in Galbraith, 1998, 98).

Hammer's roots go back to 1934 and its output has been remarkably eclectic, but it is undoubtedly its horror films that have framed its success and image. More so than Toho's special effects films, American involvement with Hammer horror was extensive, reaching from financing and distribution to scripts and casting. As Peter Arne Johnson (2021) has argued, the reasons for this are found in post-war industry legislation and Hollywood hegemony, with tax incentives like the Eadie Levy (which divided a portion of box-office rebates between exhibitors and producers if a film qualified as "British") enticing American money. The Paramount ruling similarly opened the door for British films to meet US exhibitor demand.

American involvement was present at the genesis of Hammer's horror output. When acquiring the rights to adapt the BBC's 1953 Nigel Kneale serial, *The Quatermass Experiment*, Hammer was receiving funds for its projects from American producer Robert Lippert. Lippert would also secure American distribution in exchange for Hammer's parent company, Exclusive, distributing his films in the UK (Johnson, 2021, 13). In adapting *Quatermass*, Lippert and his American partners exerted considerable control. The script was tailored towards a US market via American writer Richard Landau (Hearn & Barnes, 2007, 16), while the casting of American actor Brian Donlevy as the titular Professor Quatermass was at the insistence of Lippert and company.

Long after *The Quatermass Xperiment* (1955, Val Guest), once Hammer had properly established its horror credentials via its Frankenstein and Dracula series, American involvement remained strong. One of Robert Lippert's associates was Elliot Hyman, who would form Seven Arts Productions in 1957; it distributed several Hammer films in the US. In 1967, Seven Arts merged with Warner Bros., forming Warner Bros.-

Seven Arts. Naturally, this provided lucrative US release opportunities for Hammer, with Warner Bros.-Seven Arts exerting influence over production. However, as explored in the 2017 documentary *Hammer Horror: The Warner Bros. Years*, when the company was sold in 1969, Hammer's distribution and investment opportunities grew increasingly inconsistent. Hammer, in its most recognised form, did not survive beyond the 1970s. And while this decline was also influenced by other factors, including the departure of key staff members, competition from other British studios (such as Amicus Productions), and a wider depression in British cinema, a lack of consistent American investment/distribution hit the company hard.

American involvement, then, was integral to both the emergence of the Hammer horror brand and its commercial viability. Furthermore, it is worth noting that mere American *presence* – let alone direct involvement via financing – impacted Hammer's creative image. Firstly, the film that properly put Hammer on the map, *The Curse of Frankenstein* (1957, Terence Fisher), originated with two Americans – Max J. Rosenberg and Milton Subotsky – who eventually formed Hammer's rival, the aforementioned Amicus. In sharp correspondence with Rosenberg and Subotsky regarding their Frankenstein idea, Hammer's Michael Carreras warned against possible similarities to Universal's 1931 *Frankenstein*: "We suggest that the screenplay is checked against the original film by somebody competent to recognise the infringement of copyrights" (Kinsey, 2002, 50). Ultimately, Hammer did not proceed with Subotksy's screenplay, and a script was instead penned by Jimmy Sangster. Nevertheless, concerns persisted over potential litigation from Universal. Elliot Hyman wrote to Carreras suggesting that producer Anthony Hinds and director Terence Fisher view the Universal Frankenstein films "in order that duplication be eliminated" (Kinsey, 2002, 59). Thus, the creative approach that defined *The Curse of Frankenstein* – a film considered one of Hammer's "centres of gravity" (Hutchings in Walker, 2021, 94–95) – was steered by implicit US presence via potential copyright infringement. As Johnson (2021, 19) says, it was Hammer's aversion to litigation that ultimately produced the "house style" for which it became known.

Eventually, the massive success of Hammer's version of *Dracula* (1958, Terence Fisher) encouraged Universal to open its film library to the British studio – Universal having distributed *Dracula* in the US (Kinsey, 2002, 144–46). In turn, when *The*

Mummy (1959, Terence Fisher) was produced, screenwriter Jimmy Sangster actively used elements from Universal's mummy films of the 1930s and 1940s, such as the "scroll of life" from *The Mummy* (1932, Karl Fruend) and the swampy climax of *The Mummy's Ghost* (1944, Reginald Le Borg). This is further evidence of the significant American influence in the making of these films, both creative and financial.

Hammer's fortunes being so reliant on US capital demonstrates the centrality of the American film market and how firm its hegemony was. It therefore reinforces how the process of export and alteration for Toho's monster films was not an entirely unique phenomenon, being instead part of a wider web of global cultural flows determined in large part by Hollywood's power. However, this is not to deny the distinct and separate ways in which the films of Toho and Hammer interacted with Hollywood. For example, the signifiers of alteration are far more obvious for Godzilla films than for Hammer: Godzilla films required dubbing while Hammer's were already in English; Hammer films never had American actors added after the fact, but instead were included during production – in turn obfuscating US involvement further; cultural exchanges between Britain and the US (as historically close Western allies) were not subject to the same historical or racial dynamics that influenced the means of exchange between the US and Japan, with necessary consideration of the impact of Japan and America's then-recent oppositional history; and this specific wartime and Occupation history means that certain localisation changes are more politically charged than decisions mandated for Hammer, particularly those regarding nuclear weapons. As Steven Rawle (2022, 18–19) says when discussing cultural flows, "Lines of flow become uneven and multidirectional between different regions, industries and nations… where historical power relations are different, while acknowledging different relationships regionally and globally".

The history of Hammer Films, as the *other* major monster makers of the era, illustrates how pervasive American film interests were, and how they were very often present within the production of these films and not just in the preparation of their localised stateside release versions. In turn, this provides a wider perspective on the landscape into which Godzilla films – and indeed other Japanese science-fiction product – entered US release, placing them in a context that recognises the wider structures at play: the Paramount ruling and its impact, the opportunities for import and exhibition of overseas films, and the involvement of American studios in foreign production as indicative of Hollywood's hegemonic power.

Chapter Five: The Legacy of *Ghidorah, the Three-Headed Monster*

The legacy of *Ghidorah, the Three-Headed Monster* can be measured in a variety of ways. The film consolidated an implicit connection between all Toho monster films past and future; the many appearances of King Ghidorah throughout and outside the Godzilla series demonstrate the character's popularity and marketability, and therefore the significance of *Ghidorah* as its introductory vehicle; and Godzilla's heroism and human traits – as cemented in *Ghidorah* – provided a framework for future interactions between audience and character.

Crossover Potential and Parallels

King Kong vs. Godzilla was the first Godzilla film to pit the character against a pre-existing opponent, but *Mothra vs. Godzilla* united separate Toho monster properties, specifically. Furthermore, while *Mothra vs. Godzilla* does not directly reference the events of *Mothra*, the return of its characters (i.e., the Shobijin) suggests its connection to the Godzilla series.

Ghidorah, the Three-Headed Monster consolidated and expanded this potential for further crossovers. For example, Mothra's second appearance in a Godzilla film via *Ghidorah* (along with the Shobijin) reinforces the connection between the Godzilla series and *Mothra*; Professor Murai similarly implies connections to *Mothra vs. Godzilla* when he recalls that Godzilla and Mothra once had a fight. Rodan's inclusion naturally ties the 1956 *Rodan* to the Godzilla series as well, with the monster emerging from Mount Aso – where it was last seen in its debut film. Moreover, when Salno warns of Rodan's return, the public's reaction suggests that the monster is already well known in the world of the film.

That Mothra and Rodan have reappeared multiple times throughout the Godzilla series, in both Japanese and American films, demonstrates the lasting impact of *Ghidorah*'s unification of their separate stories.

Ghidorah's importance in this regard can be seen in the precedent it set, with monsters from isolated films turning up in subsequent Godzilla stories without need of explanation. *Destroy All Monsters* is the key example post-*Ghidorah*, with Gorosaurus (from *King Kong Escapes*), Baragon (from *Frankenstein vs. Baragon*), Manda (from *Atragon*), and Varan (from *Giant Monster Varan*) making their first appearances in the Godzilla series. Although the specifics of any narrative continuity are not addressed (for example, it is unclear whether Manda's appearance in *Destroy All Monsters* confirms any actual connection to the events of *Atragon*), the monsters themselves become unbound from their particular films and easily enter the Godzilla series. The Godzilla films, then, form the centre of Toho's genre canon, with aesthetic, tonal, and production continuities taking precedence over clearly defined narrative continuity.

With this in mind, it is worth examining the parallels that exist between the Godzilla series in the 1960s and Universal's horror films during the 1930s and 1940s. After the monsters of Universal's canon debuted in their own films, like *Dracula*, *Frankenstein*, and their subsequent sequels, 1943's *Frankenstein Meets the Wolf Man* (Roy William Neil) allowed them to meet in shared narrative spaces. Both *House of Frankenstein* (1944, Erle C. Kenton) and *House of Dracula* (1945, Erle C. Kenton) followed and mixed the Frankenstein monster, the Wolf Man, and Dracula in often incongruous but nonetheless shared stories. In turn, when these films were spoofed in *Abbott and Costello Meet Frankenstein* (1948, Charles Barton), the stage was already set for all three monsters to reunite – along with the Invisible Man at the very end. This is not unlike *Ghidorah*'s effect on the Godzilla series.

Universal's monster films are also musically linked through their use of composite scores. These were soundtracks comprised of new material that was supplemented (often considerably so) with cues and melodies from prior films which were then reworked for new sequences. Though the practice of composite scoring was not exclusive to Universal – nor its monster films – and would continue long after the studio's horror cycle of the 1930s and 1940s had ended, the shared cues and melodies aid in the merging of films and characters into shared narratives.

While Toho's monster films did not have composite scores in the same sense as Universal's horror pictures, Akira Ifukube nonetheless wrote a number of motifs that reappeared across his genre work. For example, his title track for *Giant Monster*

Ghidorah, the Three-Headed Monster

Varan would be reworked as Rodan's theme in *Ghidorah*, before becoming more generally associated with Godzilla in subsequent films. In conversations this author had with historian and scholar of Akira Ifukube, Erik Homenick, the approach was explained as follows:

> Generally speaking, Japanese composers have less time to craft film scores than their Hollywood counterparts; in Ifukube's day, it was not unheard of for composers to write, orchestrate, and record entire scores within a matter of weeks. Although Ifukube had assistants when writing his cinema scores, the vast majority of the work was his to do: write the score, orchestrate it, hire an orchestra of independent contractors, and supervise the recording sessions, which involved conducting the recorded performance.
>
> It is not clear how much time Ifukube might have had to prepare the music for *Ghidorah, the Three-Headed Monster*, but keeping in mind that film was only one of fourteen the composer worked on in 1964, logic dictates that he likely had a very limited amount of time to put everything together, probably less than one month. This likely explains why Ifukube repurposed more or less verbatim thematic material from earlier films in *Ghidorah* – it was a time-saving technique.

As Homenick says, Ifukube fully wrote his own compositions, whereas Universal's composite scores were – as the name suggests – comprised of music from several composers, including Herman Stein, Hans J. Salter, and Henry Mancini. Yet despite differences in circumstance and specifics, Ifukube's recycled melodies grant a unifying musical signature for Toho's monster properties in much the same way that Universal's composite scores do across their horror pictures. In both cases, the house style afforded by the music affirms the potential for crossover and shared stories.

Lastly, a noteworthy connection is that John Beck's US version of *King Kong vs. Godzilla* replaced portions of Ifukube's score with cues by Hans J. Salter originally composed for Universal's *Creature from the Black Lagoon* (1954, Jack Arnold). Universal itself then picked up *King Kong vs. Godzilla* for release in 1963. Two years later, Toho would produce *Frankenstein vs. Baragon*, in which actor Koji Furahata plays the Frankenstein monster with makeup reminiscent of Jack Pierce's appliances for Boris Karloff.

Looking ahead, we are arguably seeing similar crossover consolidations in the years since *Shin Godzilla* (2016, Hideaki Anno, Shinji Higuchi). The immense success of the film in Japan and the assurance of further "Shin" reboots in the form of *Shin Ultraman* (2022, Shinji Higuchi) and *Shin Kamen Rider* (2023, Hideaki Anno) has produced the "Shin Japan Heroes Universe", an ongoing collaborative project between the respective property holders of Godzilla, Ultraman, Kamen Rider, and Neon Genesis Evangelion – all properties with which Hideaki Anno has been involved. From theme-park rides and tie-in merchandise to video games and an entire marketing strategy, Godzilla, Ultraman, Kamen Rider, and Neon Genesis Evangelion are now regularly seen together as part of the collaboration. Indeed, this goes beyond the crossover potential consolidated by *Ghidorah* – which was exclusive to Toho properties – and encompasses different companies. Kamen Rider is property of Toei, while Ultraman belongs to Tsuburaya Productions, for example.

This is not to suggest that *Ghidorah* is directly responsible for the kind of crossover between these properties. It was arguably primed from inception in that the Ultraman franchise (especially in its earliest programmes) and its parent company crossed paths with Toho several times in the form of distribution arrangements and in the sharing of staff members, sound design, and monster costumes – Baragon was altered to become Pagos in *Ultra Q* (1966) and then Neronga, Magular, and Gabora in *Ultraman*, for example. Moreover, Ultraman and Kamen Rider had already appeared together in a short film made for a 1993 television special, and various stage shows have featured Godzilla with Ultraman. The screening of Ultraman compilation films alongside Godzilla titles via the Toho Champion Festivals similarly foreruns this kind of crossover. Nevertheless, the ease with which these properties mesh recalls the effortless ability for crossover that *Ghidorah* confirmed in the Godzilla series.

The Malleability of King Ghidorah

King Ghidorah remains one of the most recognisable and popular characters in Toho's monster canon, evident in its many appearances both within and outside the Godzilla series. During the original run of Godzilla films between 1954 and 1975, King Ghidorah appeared four times as a primary character and twice more via stock-footage cameos – in *Godzilla vs. Mechagodzilla* (1974, Jun Fukuda) and *Terror of Mechagodzilla*. King Ghidorah would also appear in two episodes of Toho's *Zone Fighter* (1973) television series, which took its aesthetic cues from Tsuburaya Productions' Ultraman franchise and other sources.

Although King Ghidorah made just one appearance in the second Godzilla series (between 1984 and 1995) via *Godzilla vs. King Ghidorah* (1991, Kazuki Omori), the character would appear twice as the chief villain in Toho's Mothra trilogy – made after the Godzilla series ended with *Godzilla vs. Destoroyah* (1995, Takao Okawara). In *Rebirth of Mothra* (1996, Okihiro Yoneda) and *Rebirth of Mothra III* (1998, Okihiro Yoneda), King Ghidorah received new designs and altered names (such as "Desghidorah" in the first film).

In the third Godzilla series (1999–2004), King Ghidorah made two further appearances: as a guardian protector in *Godzilla, Mothra, and King Ghidorah: Giant Monsters All-Out Attack* (2001, Shusuke Kaneko), and as the last monster Godzilla faces in *Godzilla: Final Wars* (2004, Ryuhei Kitamura). King Ghidorah has also appeared in different mediums via the third film in Polygon Pictures' anime Godzilla trilogy, *Godzilla: The Planet Eater* (2018, Kobun Shizuno & Hiroyuki Seshita). More recently, the character appeared as the chief monster villain in Legendary Pictures' *Godzilla: King of the Monsters* (2019, Michael Dougherty), the sequel to their 2014 American reimagining of the Godzilla series. The character's appearance in American entries emphasises its popularity in the US.

In Chapter Three, we discussed the malleability of King Ghidorah's character, that the monster's alien form provides a broad canvas on which different ideas can be projected. This differs from Godzilla and Mothra, for example. While the specifics of their symbolism have always changed and diverged across and within different films and contexts, Godzilla and Mothra nevertheless always carry a basic set of connotations. Godzilla is irrevocably tied to nuclear weapons; Mothra is bound to themes of transformation and rebirth. By contrast, King Ghidorah's interpretative edges appear even less defined. Given the character's recurrence throughout the series, examining a selection of its later appearances allows for an appreciation of its fluid symbolism, and therefore how the construction of its 1964 debut facilitated its enduring popularity. We shall consider four specific titles, both to focus our attention and because the films in question position King Ghidorah in unique ways.

Following *Ghidorah*, the monster immediately returned in the next Godzilla film: *Invasion of Astro-Monster*. Astronauts Glenn (Nick Adams) and Fuji (Akira Takarada) of the World Space Authority are sent to a recently discovered planet on the dark side of Jupiter, Planet X. They find a race of people forced to live underground because King Ghidorah has ravaged the planet's surface. The leader of Planet X (Yoshio Tsuchiya) offers a cure for cancer in exchange for Godzilla and Rodan; he believes the monsters will finally rid them of Ghidorah. Earth's leaders are open to the arrangement, and Godzilla and Rodan are transported to Planet X. However, the tape on which the cure for cancer is recorded actually plays an ultimatum for humanity: become a colony of Planet X or face destruction. As mankind struggles to defend itself, Godzilla, Rodan, and King Ghidorah – all under Planet X control – are unleashed upon the world.

Deceit is therefore one of the film's key elements, defining the interplanetary relations of the story. When placed in a historical context, these ideas of deception before a massive assault recall Japan's wartime actions, specifically the relations it shared with the US prior to the attack on Pearl Harbor.

For most of 1941, Japan and the US were engaged in intense diplomatic talks regarding the former's aggressive expansion in China. Dozens of proposals were submitted, rejected, revised, and re-submitted by both countries, complicated constantly by both Japanese expansion (i.e., the Japanese occupation of French Indochina in July) and global implication (Japan and the US were acutely aware of the war in Europe and of the former's obligations to the Tripartite Pact). Japanese ambassador Kichisaburo Nomura and, later, foreign minister Teijiro Toyoda tried to sustain diplomatic negotiations with Washington as pro-war voices in Tokyo grew stronger.

Takuma Melber (2021, 47–48) has argued that the fundamental disagreement over Japan's occupation of China laid bare the differences in both nation's approaches. Melber asserts that the US proposals focused on the future of their financial interests in Asia and the Pacific in the long term – hence their preoccupation with "Open Door" and "Good Neighbour" policies to promote free trade – while Japanese proposals concerned the short term, focused on recognition of Japan's conquests in China and securing access to vital resources. Japan's naval and military commanders began formulating plans for war as soon as September 1941, but the US had similarly considered pre-emptive military action even earlier in July via a potential aerial bombardment of Japanese industrial cities. These US plans were abandoned in favour of oil embargoes following Japan's occupation of Indochina (Melber, 2021, 31–42).

When Japan attacked Pearl Harbor on 7 December 1941, the cordial relations pursued by Nomura stood in contrast to the military action which had thrust the two nations into war. Even before the attack, in November 1941, Nomura lamented that he felt like a hypocrite, that he was deceiving the US (Melber, 2021, 50). This mood was galvanised when the letter announcing Japan's declaration of war against the US did not arrive until an hour after the attack. It was planned for the letter to be presented at 1pm on 7 December, around 7:30am Hawaiian time, shortly before the attack commenced. However, due to the nature of how Tokyo sent their instructions to Nomura's staff, he was unable to present the letter to Secretary of State Cordell Hull until 2pm, by which time the US was already aware.

Deception was certainly how the US characterised the events leading to Pearl Harbor, most evident in President Roosevelt's 8 December address in which he said, "the Japanese government has deliberately sought to deceive the United States by false statements and expressions of hope for continued peace". Of course, that speech should be placed in a context that remembers America's own plans for a pre-emptive attack against Japan. Moreover, the narrative of deception helped to disguise American embarrassment at having been attacked by soldiers, sailors, and airmen it considered inferior (Michener in Weglyn, 2003, 27).

The narrative of deception nevertheless took hold, and thus the deception against humanity by Planet X is arguably reminiscent of the prelude to Pearl Harbor. This connection also finds weight in the distrust that astronauts Glenn and Fuji feel after they hear Planet X's offer; both wonder if something else is at play. This is not unlike the distrust and suspicion that characterised much of the interplay between the US and Japan throughout the 1941 negotiations. If we sustain this analysis, then Planet

X, as an imperial state with plans to turn Earth into a colonial outpost, is evocative of Imperial Japan. King Ghidorah, then, is a tool of imperial conquest.

In turn, King Ghidorah's symbolism in *Astro-Monster* is essentially a more developed version of that which we discussed in *Ghidorah*: a national identity conflict made flesh. Defeating King Ghidorah and the invaders from Planet X – and therefore their evocation of Japan's wartime belligerence – suggests modern Japan moving forward. This is emphasised by American actor Nick Adams as astronaut Glenn, comfortably situating post-war Japan as an international state but also recalling Yoshikuni Igarashi's (2000, 121) analysis of *King Kong vs. Godzilla*, which highlights the foundational post-war narrative of Japan saved from itself by America. Here, American presence (implied via Glenn) works with agents of modern Japan (Fuji and others) to suppress an invader which evokes Japan's past, touching multiple post-war narratives and their functions in the process – see Chapter One. For example, post-war Japan defeating its wartime self clearly demarcates past and present, severing the ties between them and thus providing an easy distinction between the two – which is partly facilitated by American presence in the story. Thus, in *Invasion of Astro-Monster*, King Ghidorah is firstly a physical weapon of conquest and an abstract (though more detailed) means of resolving Japan's national character.

The leader of Planet X speaks with the people of Earth in *Invasion of Astro-Monster*. Producer: Tomoyuki Tanaka. Director: Ishiro Honda.

King Ghidorah would return as a tool of conquest in later sequels like *Destroy All Monsters* and *Godzilla vs. Gigan* (1972, Jun Fukuda), with the specifics of each

Ghidorah, the Three-Headed Monster

iteration altered depending on the demands of the story. In the latter, for example, King Ghidorah is used by cockroach invaders from Nebula SpaceHunter M who have escaped their polluted world to conquer Earth before mankind can commit further ecological harm. In *Godzilla vs. Gigan*, King Ghidorah as conqueror shifts from a means of separating wartime and post-war national identities, as can be read into *Invasion of Astro-Monster*, and is instead informed by Japan's pollution crisis of the 1970s – by which time the fruits of the country's post-war revival had wrought terrible environmental harm.

Nine years after *Terror of Mechagodzilla*, the Godzilla series was revived via *The Return of Godzilla*, which acted as a direct sequel to the 1954 original, ignoring all prior films. In this second series of Godzilla films, King Ghidorah appeared in 1991's *Godzilla vs. King Ghidorah*. In the film, time travellers from the twenty-third century arrive in present-day Japan with a grave warning: Godzilla will eventually return in the twenty-first century to render Japan uninhabitable. They propose returning to Lagos Island in 1944 where a group of Imperial Japanese soldiers were supposedly saved from US forces by a dinosaur – the creature which eventually became Godzilla when the US conducted its nuclear tests in the Pacific. The time travellers remove the dinosaur from Lagos Island and place it in the Bering Sea, but they secretly replace it with three small creatures called Dorats. In the present, the atom bomb has mutated the Dorats into King Ghidorah, which ravages Japan.

Contrasting with its debut appearance, wherein the character's alien origin allows for wider symbolic speculation, King Ghidorah's earthbound and deliberate origins here attach more specific meaning. King Ghidorah is again a tool of subjugation, but in a different manner pertinent to Japan's trade position in the 1980s. In this film, King Ghidorah is a weapon of Western economic warfare.

The film reveals that eventually Japan will economically supersede all other nations to become the dominant world power, buying up entire countries. The time travellers, Wilson (Chuck Wilson), Glenchiko (Richard Berger), and Emmy (Anna Nakagawa), return to present-day Japan to prevent the country's future domination. The film also features Yoshio Tsuchiya as Yasuaki Shindo. He was commanding officer of the Imperial Japanese forces on Lagos Island, and now sits as head of the Teiyo Group, a corporation which helped rebuild Japan's economy after the war; it is so powerful that it even possesses its own private nuclear submarines. Thus, the film addresses several overlapping ideas, from the extreme American "Japan Bashing" phenomenon and its relation to trade friction in the 1980s to the continuities between pre-war and post-war Japan.

US–Japan trade disputes had steadily increased since the 1970s, reaching their height in the following decade. American resentment at Japan's trade surplus against its trade deficit manifested in US sanctions and restrictions on Japanese imports, hypothetical scenarios predicting trade wars (Bailey, 1996, 143–44), an increase in racist violence against Japanese and Asian Americans (Iino, 1994, 22–25), and the deliberate invocation of wartime memory.

According to Kingston (2014, 36–37), the Japanese government strictly controlled foreign exchange for imports, effectively reserving the domestic market for domestic producers. High domestic prices then subsidised Japanese exports, creating a difficult environment for foreign exporters to break into. An increase of Japanese shares in key groups and industries, as well as the purchase of American companies by Japanese corporations, similarly angered US businesses. In the face of American sanctions and criticism, Japan voluntarily reduced its share of the US steel market and limited its exports of integrated-circuit chips in the mid-1980s (Bailey, 1996, 144). Nevertheless, a July 1987 publicity stunt saw nine US congressmen smashing a Toshiba radio on Capitol Hill after the company sold material to the Soviet Union. The sale, it was feared, would allow the Soviets to produce silent submarine propellers. To the US, the deal also highlighted the imbalance between Japan's own defence spending and its reliance on American military protection (Packard, 1987, 348).

Many US critics invoked wartime memories in their hostility toward Japan, with some implying a resurgence of Japanese imperial aggression via trade. As put by Christopher Harding (2019, 360–61), some believed Japan had "exchanged bayonet blades for sharp suits, and tanks for Toyota Corollas". Beyond the US, however, there were serious assertions of a new Japanese imperialism across Southeast Asia in the 1970s (Bailey, 1996, 123–28), given Japan's significant investments and trade imbalances across the region. Japan took advantage of low-wage labour and low-cost manufacturing (Urata in Ito & Krueger, 1993, 275), leveraging the Asian Development Bank for greater economic penetration, and was encouraged by the US to take up an active role in regional geopolitics along ideological, anti-communist lines (Singh, 2002, 281–85). In Indonesia, where protests were held against Japanese economic imperialism in 1974, trade imbalances with Japan came in tandem with financial aid that benefitted Japanese industry (Roderick, 1974, 2). Japan's direct investments in Asia, Europe, and Latin America continued throughout this period as financial controls were liberalised, with Japanese-owned plants and factories established in South Korea, Taiwan, and elsewhere. According to Bailey (1996, 123), Japan accounted for 64% of all foreign investment in South Korea in 1976, which is reminiscent of the film's notion that Japan eventually buys entire countries.

It should be emphasised, then, that American suggestions of a resurgent Japanese imperialism were obviously not grounded in any genuine, *ethical* concerns over Japanese economic dominance or its neocolonial extraction in the post-war era. Rather, American invocation of wartime memory was designed to structure and justify contemporary US antagonism toward Japan and the challenges presented to its financial interests.

Godzilla vs. King Ghidorah runs parallel to this context, specifically in relation to US resentment at Japan's trade position. Although writer–director Kazuki Omori envisioned Glenchiko as Russian (Homenick, 2019), he and Wilson effectively appear as Westerners. They therefore evoke contemporary American sentiments in their goal of preventing Japan's future economic domination.

Concurrently, Emmy's character prevents the film from becoming a mere nationalist-capitalist fantasy, one in which those who try to undermine Japan's economic power are clearly enemies. When King Ghidorah is unleashed, she argues with her comrades. She asserts that their plan was originally to extort a different path out of present-day Japan to prevent the country's future colonial–economic domination, but that Wilson and Glenchiko are simply letting the monster run rampant. She does not cede ground about the scale and severity of Japan's future empire, nor of the need to thwart it. In turn, Wilson and Glenchiko's gleeful use of King Ghidorah reads as vindictive rather than righteous, like an exaggerated version of America's self-interested trade threats. Furthermore, a scene toward the film's end, set in 2204, reveals that Japan – in at least one version of the future – is indeed eventually destroyed by Godzilla as predicted.

Time travellers from the twenty-third century arrive in present-day Japan with grave warnings. *Godzilla vs King Ghidorah*. Producer: Shogo Tomiyama. Director: Kazuki Omori.

Emmy's concern over Japan's future economic hegemony brings us to Yasuaki Shindo. As commanding officer of the Imperial Japanese forces on Lagos Island in 1944, he witnessed the dinosaur from which Godzilla mutated. The creature seemingly attacked and destroyed a US invasion force, thus Shindo believes it saved his life. His ascendancy in post-war Japan has obvious precedent, from pre-war political figures like Nobusuke Kishi to corporations and projects which saw their start or gains via Japan's imperialism (see chapters One and Three). Later in the film, Godzilla properly returns. It is theorised that a sunken Soviet submarine in the Bering Sea accidentally mutated the dinosaur, and one of Shindo's nuclear submarines is deliberately sent to revive Godzilla so that it will fight King Ghidorah.

Shindo meets the dinosaur from Lagos Island again, though now it is Godzilla and further irradiated by his submarine; the monster peers in at him through the window of his Shinjuku skyscraper. Tears well in Shindo's eyes as he remembers the sacrifice he ascribed to the dinosaur. As Akira Ifukube's moving score draws to a close, Godzilla unleashes its atomic breath. Shindo is obliterated.

Shindo and Godzilla are both products of the war, but also *post-war* Japan. Shindo's ascension and wealth were, as is implied, by-products of Japan's post-war development, and are therefore implicitly entangled in layers of influence from the US Occupation to the country's strategic position in a Cold War environment. In this film, Godzilla is ultimately the product of Shindo, deliberately mutated further by one of the latter's submarines. Shindo, standing amid the spoils of his post-war rise, looks out at another product of his material gain when he locks eyes with Godzilla. Whether or not we are to believe Shindo's assertion that the dinosaur on Lagos Island deliberately saved him and his men, his actions have further transformed it into a terrifying creature. When Godzilla kills Shindo, it reads like an act of vengeance; but what kind of vengeance? If Godzilla indeed protected Shindo as he believes, is the monster – as the wartime phantom – betrayed by Shindo's indulgence in the fruits of American investment? Or, perhaps Shindo has totally misread the monster all along, foolishly projecting his nationalism and wartime codes onto a creature that was simply protecting its territory. If so, Godzilla's violent reaction to Shindo is like a statement that his wartime belief *and* post-war wealth – which are linked – have ultimately produced nothing but destruction via (literal and figurative) monstrous embodiment. The Godzilla–Shindo relationship reflects the continuities and change that characterise post-war Japan, while Omori's cluttered script leaves room for myriad interpretations.

King Ghidorah, as a tool of economic challenge motivated by Western unease at Japanese influence, faces a Godzilla inherently tied to a single man's meteoric post-war financial success, ultimately leaving no definitive resolution to the discourses upon which the film hinges.

Considering both the film's ideas and the historical context that frames them, it should be mentioned that Japan's "bubble economy" had effectively burst by 1992 and a decade of stagnation and economic hardship for millions of people followed. In 1998, Yoichi Funabashi (27) wrote that, "Japanese business has already started to withdraw from the world. Foreign direct investment to Asia is slowing down... Fujitsu has just closed a semiconductor plant within British Prime Minister Tony Blair's Sedgefield constituency".

CONSTELLATIONS

Following *Godzilla vs. King Ghidorah*, Toho continued with *Godzilla vs. Mothra*, which sees Godzilla's return coincide with the awakening of Battra, a dark inverse of Mothra bound to punish mankind for its environmental harm. Godzilla, spawn of nuclear pollution, faces Battra, sent by Earth itself for vengeance against humanity's ecological hubris. Mothra is caught in the middle, connected to the Cosmos (the new iteration of the Shobijin), and embodying a sense of environmental balance between mankind and the planet.

After Toho ended its second Godzilla series in 1995, a trilogy of Mothra films for children commenced, and *Godzilla vs. Mothra*'s explicit environmental concerns returned in 1996's *Rebirth of Mothra*. This first film is worthy of particular examination in how it uses King Ghidorah as its chief villain.

In a reimagining of the Shobijin, *Rebirth of Mothra* establishes three sisters who are the last of the Elias, a race of people who lived in harmony with Mothra and her species millions of years ago. When Desghidorah ("Death Ghidorah") arrived from outer space to drain the Earth's energy, Mothra and the Elias fought to contain it, sealing the monster away deep underground. However, the conflict wiped out the Elias' civilisation and left Mothra as the last of her kind. In the present, a logging company in Hokkaido finds a strange medallion set into a large boulder – it is the seal that locked Ghidorah away. Two of the three sisters, Moll (Megumi Kobayashi) and Lora (Sayaka Yamaguchi), are aware of the imminent threat, but so is their villainous sister, Belvera (Aki Hano). She wants the seal removed so that Desghidorah will reawaken and destroy mankind. When the monster is released, it proceeds to drain the Earth's energy, turning Hokkaido's lush forests to wasteland.

In reinstating King Ghidorah – via Desghidorah – as an extra-terrestrial creature, *Rebirth of Mothra* openly recycles ideas from *Ghidorah, the Three-Headed Monster*. Just as King Ghidorah ravaged Venus centuries ago in *Ghidorah*, Desghidorah is also a planet killer. The monster is said to have travelled from world to world, draining them of power, before arriving on Earth. *Rebirth of Mothra* uses King Ghidorah's broad symbolic canvas (again facilitated by its alien origin) to address environmental damage. The awakening of Desghidorah brings with it the destruction of vast natural spaces. However, the film does not ascribe responsibility to the monster. Its release is made possible only by human action. This notion is delivered via Yuichi Goto (Kenjiro Nashimoto), who works for the logging company that removed the Elias' seal.

Goto's character exists in a dysfunctional family dynamic, working away from home and leaving his wife, Makiko (Hitomi Takahashi), to look after their two quarrelling children. In their analysis of the film, Sean Rhoads and Brooke McCorkle (2018, 168-69) draw links between the strained family relations at the film's beginning and the deforestation with which Goto is involved. While fighting against Desghidorah, the family members rekindle their relationships. The film's end sees the family unit secure, with Mothra having revitalised the decimated forests. Rhoads and McCorkle argue that "Once stability in the family structure is achieved, it becomes possible for humanity to achieve balance in its relationship with nature". It is within a wider connection between familial and environmental harmony that Rhoads and McCorkle place *Rebirth of Mothra*, recycling similar ideas from *Godzilla vs. Mothra*, which also sees a troubled family dynamic unfold in tandem with its ecological crisis.

Desghidorah signals environmental harm in general but also serves more specific functions in the narrative. Firstly, Desghidorah's defeat forms part of the family reconciliation. Secondly, Desghidorah allows for themes intrinsic to the Mothra character to reappear. During the film, Mothra is mortally injured by Desghidorah and escapes with her offspring to the sea. However, her wounds are too great, and she sinks into the deep. The larval Mothra then undergoes metamorphosis and emerges as an adult; it is in this form that the new Mothra defeats Desghidorah. So, Desghidorah's destructive aggression ultimately necessitates Mothra's key tenets of transformation and rebirth, which are necessary for resolution – and specifically environmental resolution in this film.

As a point of interest, the inverse of *Rebirth of Mothra* is presented in Legendary Pictures' *Godzilla: King of the Monsters*. In the film, King Ghidorah is a space monster that arrived on Earth centuries ago, now locked away beneath Antarctica. Instead of Ghidorah awakening to drain Earth's energy via environmental destruction, the monster is deliberately released by a militant environmentalist group to *return* the Earth to a more ecologically sound state. These events are also framed by a troubled family dynamic that exists parallel to the monster conflict.

Rebirth of Mothra and its two sequels were produced during the "lost decade" of Japan's economic stagnation. In April 2001, Junichiro Koizumi vowed to restructure the economy via neoliberal reform and swept to power as prime minister and LDP leader, enjoying 80% support in opinion polls (Tamamoto, 2001, 33); his economic platform has drawn comparison to both Ronald Reagan and Margaret Thatcher (Kingston, 2014, 29). In August 2001, four months before *Godzilla, Mothra, and King Ghidorah: Giant Monsters All-Out Attack* was theatrically released (henceforth referred to as "GMK" for brevity), Junichiro Koizumi visited Yasukuni Shrine in Tokyo.

Yasukuni Shrine was established in 1869 to commemorate Japan's war dead who brought about the Meiji Restoration and subsequent imperial expansion. The Shrine also lists Taiwanese and Korean soldiers forced to fight for Imperial Japan during World War II (Ryu, 2007, 708), the families of whom have requested that their names be removed. It has caused further and specific offence because 14 Class A war criminals were enshrined there in 1978, raising questions about Japan's relationship to its own history whenever visits are undertaken by prime ministers. Such visits also evoke memories of Shinto as it was used within the Imperial apparatus, when it was the state religion and functioned as part and affirmation of the *kokutai*. Modern state visits naturally call into question the separation of religion from the government as written in Japan's post-war constitution.

While criticism exists within Japan from left-wing groups, Yasukuni Shrine has prompted international outcry from the country's immediate neighbours who were subjected to Imperial Japanese aggression, including China and Korea. With the Shrine's history and use intertwined with Imperial expansion following the Meiji Restoration, not least the enshrinement of war criminals, official visits to Yasukuni have jeopardised and harmed relations with Japan's neighbours. As Yongwook Ryu (2007, 710) explains,

> Yasukuni is not merely a religious site but, more importantly, an ideologically loaded institution where the war dead are mourned and appropriated for political ends. The shrine stands as the symbol of expansionist nationalism and an authoritarian vision of domestic social order. Given this history and these functions, it is not hard to see why Yasukuni means so much to conservative nationalists, why

it is so hated by the political left, and why the Koreans and Chinese have difficulty tolerating visits to the shrine by Japanese prime ministers.

As Ryu references, the matter is equally steeped in domestic political movements. The LDP maintains links with numerous right-wing organisations, several of which send representatives to parliament as politicians, and these groups and their members have advocated for official visits to Yasukuni Shrine (Shibuichi, 2005, 201–02).

While prime ministers had visited the Shrine privately in years prior, Yasuhiro Nakasone prompted outcry in 1985 when he announced that his visit would be official. Although criticism from within and outside Japan had existed for earlier Yasukuni visits, Nakasone's 1985 announcement stirred widespread condemnation. As reported in the *Los Angeles Times* on 16 August 1985, a Beijing foreign-ministry official said in the preceding days that, "an official visit to the Yasukuni Shrine, which commemorates a number of Japanese war criminals, would hurt the feelings of both the Chinese and Japanese peoples who suffered at the hands of the militarists". Following the visit, over 1,000 Beijing and Qinghua University students conducted mass protests (Shibuichi, 2005, 206–07).

Although an outspoken nationalist, Nakasone tried to mend Sino-Japanese relations with an unsuccessful request for the Yasukuni Shrine administration to un-enshrine the war criminals (Shibuichi, 2005, 207–09). By contrast, Junichiro Koizumi visited several times during his tenure – the first occasion being 13 August 2001. Previous prime ministers between Nakasone and Koizumi generally steered clear of official visits to avoid international scrutiny, and Koizumi's pilgrimage once again sparked criticism both within and outside of Japan. His visit was set to be 15 August to coincide with the anniversary of Japan's surrender but was brought forward in response to Chinese and South Korean outcry and the urging of his own ministers (Tamamoto, 2001, 33–34). Furthermore, one of Koizumi's campaign slogans was "I visit the Yasukuni Shrine regardless of what happens" (Shibuichi, 2005, 210).

In his speech at the 2005 Asian–African Summit, Koizumi spoke of Japan's war record: "Japan, through its colonial rule and aggression, caused tremendous damage and suffering to the people of many countries, particularly to those of Asian nations.

Japan squarely faces these facts of history in a spirit of humility" (Ryu, 2007, 713). This forms the basis on which Koizumi (like many Japanese conservatives) claims to view Yasukuni, that visits to the Shrine are not to honour individuals – such as the enshrined war criminals – but the collective dead and to thank them for their sacrifice upon which modern Japan enjoys its peace and prosperity (Tamamoto, 2001, 34). However, as Ryu notes, Yasukuni cannot be disconnected from Japan's imperialism, and Koizumi's speech sits hypocritically beside broader conservative movements in Japan which have attempted to diminish or deny its war crimes. For example, Japanese school textbooks were revised in the 1980s to downplay Japan's aggression against China (Bailey, 1996, 156–57; Miyamoto, 2012, 44). More recently, J. Mark Ramseyer's discredited claims (Morris-Suzuki, 2021) that "comfort women" voluntarily engaged in contracted sex work (denying Japan's violent enforcement of sexual slavery) have been celebrated by Japanese nationalists, including LDP politicians who have, as in 2021, approvingly brought up Ramseyer's work in Diet sessions (Schieder, 2021).

These examples, like the state visits to Yasukuni Shrine and their associated discourses of international reaction and domestic implication, raise questions about Japan's relationship with itself, its imperial past and its present legacies, and its neighbours who were subjected to that imperialism. These questions foreground director Shusuke Kaneko's perspective in *GMK*, in which he offers an answer: Japan must not forget the sins of its past or the suffering of those killed during the war.

In *GMK*, Godzilla is the living embodiment of all who died in the Pacific theatre during the Second World War (Chinese, American, and Japanese alike), returned to enact vengeance against a Japan that has forgotten their suffering. Three guardian monsters, earth deities which protect not simply Japan but the very land itself, awaken to fight Godzilla: Baragon, Mothra, and King Ghidorah. Explaining his idea to Norman England (2021, 73), Kaneko said that Godzilla returns because the Japanese have "forgotten the sins of their fathers and that affluence and luxury have made them complacent".

For the first and – so far – only time in the series, King Ghidorah takes on a heroic position in relation to Godzilla. Meanwhile, Godzilla is overtly presented as vindictive, with scenes of destruction emphasising loss of life. Ghidorah, Mothra, and Baragon harm Godzilla but are not strong enough to defeat it. Stopping Godzilla is left to the film's human cast, led by reporter Yuri Tachibana (Chiharu Niiyama) and her father, Admiral Tachibana (Ryudo Uzaki). Thus, while *GMK*'s spotlight on Japan's past is framed by monsters, they do not offer resolution. Kaneko suggests that only Japan's people, as reflected by the film's cast, can do that.

Admiral Tachibana also remarks that a soldier's greatest honour is to have never seen battle, which is indicative of Kaneko's wider outlook on Japanese militarism. In a 2022 interview, Kaneko explained that he imagined the world of *GMK* as one without the US–Japan Security Treaty, and that the Japan of the film maintains a military but only for self-defence. In the same interview, Kaneko spoke of his belief that while Japan can maintain its Self Defence Force for defence only, the right of "collective self-defence" – referring to military action taken outside Japan in co-ordination with other nations – should be denied. Elaborating on this point, the director (in Kimura, 2022a, 74) said,

> If exercising the right to collective defence is denied and we cannot participate in other countries' wars, then I think having military power for defence only is fine. But I cannot agree with the exercising of the right to collective defence being approved by the cabinet and the Self Defence Forces being gradually recognised in the Constitution. [The constitutional] "Renunciation of War" would no longer be protected.

Article 9 of Japan's constitution states that the country will never maintain "land, sea, and air forces, as well as other war potential". It also renounces the threat or use of force "as means of settling international disputes". Throughout the post-war era, however, the LDP has repeatedly pushed at its semantic edges. In 1992, for example, Japan enacted a UN "peacekeeping" law enabling the deployment of the SDF overseas. In the following years, the US and Japan reworked the terms of the US–Japan Security Treaty to further expand the scope of US–Japan operations (Sakamoto, 2001, 23). Furthermore, two years after *GMK*, Junichiro Koizumi authorised the deployment of Japanese troops to Iraq to support the US in its invasion. And, in 2014, the administration of Shinzo Abe (grandson to Nobusuke Kishi) would pass a cabinet decision allowing Japan to exercise the right to "collective self-defence" under certain circumstances, promulgated in 2015. In turn, Kaneko's concerns over "collective self-defence" and its implications for Japanese remilitarisation find their meaning, naturally fitting into wider conversations that include the Yasukuni Shrine, relations with Japan's neighbours, Japan's active collaboration in upholding American imperialist hegemony, and reflections on Japan's imperial past and its links to the present. *GMK* contributes to these conversations, warning Japan not to forget its history.

King Ghidorah's place in the story again emphasises the malleability of the character, taking on heroic traits and fighting against the personification of modern Japan's hubris. More significant is how Ghidorah's inclusion illustrates the popularity and marketability of the character. Kaneko had first wanted to include Kamakiras (the giant praying mantis from *Son of Godzilla*), but executive producer Shogo Tomiyama explained that Toho did not want another insect creature, having recently used one in *Godzilla x Megaguirus* (2000, Masaaki Tezuka). Kaneko then planned to use Varan, Baragon, and Anguirus but found that none of his peers at a grade-school reunion could remember those characters (Kaneko in Kimura, 2022a, 74). Then, after the poor box-office performance of *Godzilla x Megaguirus*, it was decided that King Ghidorah and Mothra would replace Anguirus and Varan to improve *GMK*'s financial prospects. Shogo Tomiyama (in Kimura, 2022a, 71) recalled,

> It was because of the business result of *Godzilla x Megaguirus*. Something had to be done. At that time, we were thinking that GMK would be the very last Godzilla movie, and the company requested it to be an "all-star" movie. To be honest, I was disappointed about this request. I liked Mr. Kaneko's monster ideas, and we already used both Mothra and King Ghidorah just recently.

Tomiyama's disappointment notwithstanding, the inclusion of King Ghidorah highlights how recognisable and popular the character was – having become a financial buoyancy aid for the series along with Mothra.

Invasion of Astro-Monster, *Godzilla vs. King Ghidorah*, *Rebirth of Mothra*, and *GMK* all demonstrate the flexibility of King Ghidorah's meaning. The creature's alien image has been a tool to confront myriad concerns and ideas, specific to the contexts in which these sequels were made – be it Japan's new image in 1964 or environmental

Ghidorah, the Three-Headed Monster

destruction. Even when given more defined interpretive edges through explicitly earthbound origins, the character's potential for meaning remains far-reaching – from a reflection of Japan's economic position in the 1980s to a framing device for conversations about its past and present. These factors ultimately assert the significance of *Ghidorah, the Three-Headed Monster* in introducing the character, and how its execution has allowed for repeated and varied employment.

Relating to Godzilla

As mentioned in Chapter Three, Godzilla, Rodan, Mothra, and company have always been open to audience connection from their first appearances. However, *Ghidorah* took this capacity for connection and made it overt in the deliberate and pronounced anthropomorphism of the Godzilla character, from the depiction of motive and emotion in the "monster talk" scene to the use of Haruo Nakajima's own physicality in his performance as Godzilla.

After *Ghidorah*, every subsequent film of the 1960s and 1970s continued to anthropomorphise Godzilla. *Invasion of Astro-Monster* sees Godzilla perform a victory dance (based on the popular 1962–69 *Osomatsu-kun* manga) after defeating King Ghidorah on Planet X; *Son of Godzilla* sees Godzilla become a father, and both father and son (Minilla) behave in a manner that leads reporter Goro Maki (Akira Kubo) to compare Godzilla to a strict parent; *Terror of Mechagodzilla* also sees Godzilla make an appearance precisely when two young boys are imperilled. The character moves from a semi-heroic (if not somewhat neutral) position in the mid-1960s, defeating invaders and antagonistic monsters but never totally losing mankind's fear, to a firmly heroic one by the 1970s. Ten years after *Ghidorah*, Godzilla was effectively on Japan's side in the fight against new threats. This is *Ghidorah*'s legacy in action, having confirmed that Godzilla's character could evolve, and thus opening the door for that evolution to continue – in line with wider industrial contexts which demanded the series change (see Chapter Two).

With *Ghidorah* having structured audience engagement, it was cemented as the original series went on. Afterwards, every subsequent Godzilla series utilised that structure for emotional engagement at one point or another. Individual characters in these films similarly further audience connection. Yasuaki Shindo's relationship with the character in *Godzilla vs. King Ghidorah* is obvious, but more prominent is Miki Saegusa (Megumi Odaka), a returning character in the 1990s films who shares a psychic link with Godzilla. Throughout those films, Saegusa often acts as a conduit for Godzilla (and its offspring), furthering audience engagement and attachment.

The use of Godzilla's offspring in films like *Godzilla vs. Mechagodzilla* (1993, Takao Okawara), *Godzilla vs. SpaceGodzilla* (1994, Kensho Yamashita), and especially *Godzilla vs. Destoroyah* frames Godzilla as a parent and then imperils its children to elicit audience sympathy – essentially reworking the emotional devices of *Son of Godzilla* but with different tonal and stylistic choices. This engagement is taken a step further in *Destoroyah*, which sees Godzilla jr. killed before the adult Godzilla also dies – melting down in a fiery demise. Akira Ifukube's melodramatic score works in tandem with Miki Saegusa's tears to provoke an emotional rise.

While these examples of audience connection are, of course, also a result of specific elements unique to the individual films in question, they are similarly traceable to *Ghidorah, the Three-Headed Monster*. Again, the character transformation displayed in that film and (importantly) the explicit recognition of Godzilla's emotional capabilities by the human cast (such as Shindo saying the monsters are "as stupid as human beings") explicates and structures the possibility for further connection found in later entries.

Such connection is also present in the US-made *Godzilla* (2014, Gareth Edwards). In one scene, a battered Godzilla, weak from its battle with giant creatures called M.U.T.O.s (massive unidentified terrestrial organisms), makes eye contact with a soldier (Aaron Taylor-Johnson). The moment is brief but noteworthy, highlighted by the film's overall thesis that these monsters reveal mankind's arrogance and insignificance. Similarly, at the film's end, Godzilla wades triumphantly out to sea as crowds cheer and others look on in awe. In these moments, Godzilla is rendered as a character with which the human cast engage and/or identify. The development of the Godzilla character in *Ghidorah* has ultimately influenced not just subsequent Japanese productions but clearly those made elsewhere as well.

Just as these examples illustrate the legacy of *Ghidorah*, they also highlight the vital contributions of its creators. That Shinichi Sekizawa penned and/or contributed to seven of the eight Godzilla films made in the 1960s, and that those films began, developed, and sustained Godzilla's character transformation, speaks to his importance in influencing the legacy of the series – and how audiences perceive the character. In giving physical form, motion, and direction to that character shift, Haruo Nakajima and Eiji Tsuburaya are similarly integral. Furthermore, as King Ghidorah ultimately allowed for Godzilla to distinguish itself as a heroic force, those who designed, influenced, and physically brought it to life – Akira Watanabe, Keizo Murase, Teizo Toshimitsu, Keiko Suzuki, and Shoichi Hirose among them – are also of paramount importance.

Closing Words

Toho's most recent Godzilla film, *Godzilla Minus One* (2023, Takashi Yamazaki), was financially and critically successful. The project's director, Takashi Yamazaki, is no stranger to King Ghidorah; Yamazaki helmed an immersive amusement park ride in 2021 which featured Godzilla battling its three-headed adversary. While King Ghidorah does not feature in *Minus One*, the character's use in the 2021 ride is a reminder of its popularity. King Ghidorah remains as familiar and recognisable as ever, revealing once more the significance of its 1964 debut film.

More than just an introductory vehicle for a popular character, *Ghidorah, the Three-Headed Monster* marked both massive change and perceptible continuity for the Godzilla series. The film confirmed new directions in style and tone, with Godzilla's character developing in a friendlier direction. At the same time, the film retains and develops ideas and themes from prior Toho science-fiction films. Trust between human characters gives way to trust between monsters; monsters shift from being the source of narrative crisis to the means of its resolution. In turn, *Ghidorah* is also part of the narrative of change in post-war Japan, made particularly salient by its proximity to the 1964 Tokyo Olympics. Carefully constructed images of recovery and stability were asserted on the world stage, wartime enemy now a model of "progress". Godzilla similarly shed its monstrous visage and began a journey toward friend and ally, obscuring the historical tensions and violence which had originally animated both its character and debut film. A new image of Japan, a new image of Godzilla.

The film's own production mirrors these changes, with Haruo Nakajima's performance taking on more of his own physicality as encouraged by Eiji Tsuburaya. The picture's special effects, intricate in their construction and precise in their execution, reveal the dedication and talent of the artists who brought it to life. Though the remarkable craftsmanship involved in *Ghidorah*'s production can be found throughout Toho's genre canon, the film is nonetheless a brilliant example of the ingenuity, skill, and artistry of its time.

The film's 1965 US release helps us historically situate the Godzilla series' global success, but also prompts wider examination of the American market for foreign films. Looking at American influence in the cultural longevity of similar genre outputs – like those of Hammer Films in Britain – reveals threads shared with comparable productions in a market dominated and therefore often dictated by Hollywood.

Finally, as discussed in this last chapter, we can understand and approach *Ghidorah*'s firm legacy. For as long as the Godzilla series remains a viable source of revenue for Toho, King Ghidorah will endure as a familiar sight – whether in the form of merchandise, amusement park rides, or future film appearances. Each time, the character's symbolic edges shift and morph, highlighting the interpretative flexibility allowed by its initial extra-terrestrial origins, and reflective of its perennial popularity.

The fifth Godzilla movie, *Ghidorah, the Three-Headed Monster*, is an endlessly entertaining film that marks influential changes for the series, ingenious special effects, and reflections of prominent post-war narratives.

> *It would be a bad situation if that creature came here to Earth.*
>
> *It's worse, because he's arrived.*

Bibliography

Texts

Anderson, Joseph L. & Richie, Donald (1982). *The Japanese Film: Art and Industry* (Expanded Edition). Princeton, New Jersey: Princeton University Press.

Aoki, Shinya [Editor] (2012). *SFX Films Art Director Yasuyuki Inoue.* Japan: Kinema Junpo Co., Ltd.

Arkoff, Sam & Trubo, Richard (1992). *Flying through Hollywood by the Seat of My Pants.* New York: Carol Publishing Group.

Bailey, Paul J. (1996). *Postwar Japan: 1945 to the Present.* Oxford, UK, and Cambridge, Massachusetts: Blackwell Publishers.

Balio, Tino (2010). *The Foreign Film Renaissance on American Screens, 1946–1973.* Madison, Wisconsin: The University of Wisconsin Press.

Barr, Jason (2016). *The Kaiju Film.* Jefferson, North Carolina, and London: McFarland & Company, Inc., Publishers.

Bernardi, J. & Ogawa, S. (2020). *Routledge Handbook of Japanese Cinema.* Oxfordshire: Taylor & Francis.

Brock, David (1989). *The Theory and Practice of Japan-Bashing in The National Interest,* No. 17, pp. 29–40. Center for the National Interest.

Choi, Deokhyo (2017). *Fighting the Korean War in Pacifist Japan: Korean and Japanese Leftist Solidarity and American Cold War Containment in Critical Asian Studies,* Vol. 49, No. 4, pp. 546–68. Routledge.

Chun, Jayson Makato (2007). *"A Nation of a Hundred Million Idiots"? A Social History of Japanese Television, 1953-1973.* New York & London: Routledge.

Crandol, Michael (2019). *Godzilla vs. Dracula: Hammer Horror Films in Japan* in *Cinephile,* Vol. 13, No. 1, pp. 18–23.

Dower, John (2000). *Embracing Defeat: Japan in the Aftermath of World War II.* London: Penguin Books.

Driscoll, Mark (2010). *Absolute Erotic, Absolute Grotesque: The Living, Dead, and Undead in Japan's Imperialism, 1895–1945.* Durham and London: Duke University Press.

Endo, Sekkei [Editor] (1985a). *Toho SF SFX Movie Series Vol. 2: Mothra/Mothra vs. Godzilla.* Tokyo: Toho Co., Ltd. Division of Published Product Promotion Office.

Endo, Sekkei [Editor] (1985b). *Toho SF SFX Movie Series Vol. 4: Atragon/Gorath/Space Monster Dogora.* Tokyo: Toho Co., Ltd. Division of Published Product Promotion Office.

England, Norman (2021). *Behind the Kaiju Curtain: A Journey onto Japan's Biggest Film Sets.* New York: Awai Books.

Ezawa, Takashi [Issuer] (2016). *Movie Treasure Collection: Along with Godzilla*, Toho SFX VIP Interviews. Tokyo: Yoshensha Co. Ltd.

Fritzsche, Sonja [Editor] (2021). *The Liverpool Companion to World Science Fiction Film.* Liverpool, UK: Liverpool University Press.

Frydman, Joshua (2022). *The Japanese Myths: A Guide to Gods, Heroes and Spirits.* London: Thames & Hudson Ltd.

Fujiki, Hideaki & Phillips, Alastair (2020). *The Japanese Cinema Book.* London and New York: Bloomsbury Publishing Plc.

Funabashi, Yoichi (1998). *Tokyo's Depression Diplomacy in Foreign Affairs*, Vol. 77, No. 6, pp. 26–36. Council on Foreign Relations.

Galbraith, Stuart IV (1994). *Japanese Science Fiction, Fantasy and Horror Films: A Critical Analysis of 103 Features Released in the United States, 1950–1992.* Jefferson, North Carolina, and London: McFarland & Company, Inc., Publishers.

Galbraith, Stuart IV (1996). *The Japanese Filmography: A Complete Reference Work to 209 Filmmakers and the More than 1250 Films Released in the United States, 1900–1994.* Jefferson, North Carolina, and London: McFarland & Company, Inc., Publishers.

Galbraith, Stuart IV (1998). *Monsters are Attacking Tokyo! The Incredible World of Japanese Fantasy Films.* Venice, CA: Feral House.

Garon, Sheldon & Machlachlan, Patricia L. [Editors] (2006). *The Ambivalent Consumer: Questioning Consumption in East Asia and the West.* Ithaca and London: Cornell University Press.

Harding, Christopher (2019). *Japan Story: In Search of a Nation, 1850 to the Present.* Milton Keynes: Penguin Random House UK.

Hearn, Marcus & Barnes, Alan (2007). *The Hammer Story: The Authorised History of Hammer Films* (Revised Edition). London: Titan Books.

Heffernan, Kevin (2004). *Ghouls, Gimmicks, and Gold: Horror Films and the American Movie Business, 1953–1968.* Durham and London: Duke University Press.

Hirano, Kyoko (1992). *Mr. Smith Goes to Tokyo: Japanese Cinema under the American Occupation, 1945–1952.* Washington and London: Smithsonian Institution Press.

Homenick, Brett (2016). *NATSUKI ON NATSUKI! Actor Yosuke Natsuki Opens Up About His Remarkable Career in Show Business!* https://vantagepointinterviews.com/2016/02/18/natsuki-on-natsuki-actor-yosuke-natsuki-opens-up-about-his-remarkable-career-in-show-business/ [Accessed 19/11/21]

Homenick, Brett (2017). *REFLECTIONS OF HIROSHI KOIZUMI! The Toho Star Opens Up About His Career!* https://vantagepointinterviews.com/2017/05/13/reflections-of-hiroshi-koizumi-the-toho-star-opens-up-about-his-career/ [Accessed 19/11/21]

Homenick, Brett (2018a). *MEMORIES OF JAPAN'S MASTER MONSTERMAKER! Keizo Murase Shares the Secrets of the World's Greatest Kaiju!* https://vantagepointinterviews.com/2018/05/23/

memories-of-japans-master-monster-maker-keizo-murase-shares-the-secrets-of-the-worlds-greatest-kaiju/ [Accessed 19/11/21]

Homenick, Brett (2018b). *A VOICE ACTOR'S VOICE ACTOR! Larry Robinson on His Dubbing Work at Titra!* https://vantagepointinterviews.com/2018/06/30/a-voice-actors-voice-actor-larry-robinson-on-his-dubbing-work-at-titra/ [Accessed 18/3/22]

Homenick, Brett (2019). *REIMAGINING GODZILLA FOR THE HEISEI ERA! Kazuki Omori on Updating Godzilla for a New Generation!* https://vantagepointinterviews.com/2019/07/30/reimagining-godzilla-for-the-heisei-era-kazuki-omori-on-updating-godzilla-for-a-new-generation/ [Accessed 16/2/22]

Homenick, Brett (2021). *THE MASTERFUL MAKER OF MONSTER BEAMS! Sadao Iizuka on His Early Life and Career at Toho!* https://vantagepointinterviews.com/2021/12/12/the-masterful-maker-of-monster-beams-sadao-iizuka-on-his-early-life-and-career-at-toho/ [Accessed 2/2/22]

Hood, Christopher (2006). *Shinkansen: From Bullet Train to Symbol of Modern Japan.* London and New York: Routledge.

Igarashi, Yoshikuni (2000). *Bodies of Memory: Narratives of War in Postwar Japanese Culture, 1945–1970.* Princeton and Oxford: Princeton University Press.

Iino, Masako (1994). *Asian Americans Under the Influence of "Japan Bashing" in American Studies International*, Vol. 32, No. 1, pp. 17–30. Mid-America American Studies Association.

Iizuka, Sadao & Matsumoto, Hajime (2016). *A Man Who Has Been Drawing Rays: The Legend of Sadao Iizuka.* Tokyo: Yosensha Co., Ltd.

Ishii, Hiroto & Hirai, Yutaro [Editors] (2012). *Complete Book of Toho SFX Films.* Tokyo, Japan: Village Books.

Ito, Takatoshi & Krueger, O. Anne [Editors] (1993). *Trade and Protectionism.* Chicago: University of Chicago Press.

Jancovich, Mark [Editor] (2002). *The Horror Film Reader.* London and New York: Routledge.

Johnson, Peter Arne (2021). *Demystifying Hammer: The Influence of Transnational Hollywood Financing in Monstrum*, Issue 4, pp. 7–22. Published in Montréal, Québec by the Montréal Monstrum Society.

Kalat, David (2010). *A Critical History and Filmography of Toho's Godzilla Series* (Second Edition). Jefferson, North Carolina, and London: McFarland & Company, Inc., Publishers.

Kaneda, Masumi (2018). *The Venusian Fortune Teller – Ghidorah The Three-Headed Monster First Script – How the Legend of the Three-Headed Dragon Ghidorah Started in Special Effects Treasure*, Vol. 8, pp. 218–22. Tokyo: Yoshensha Co. Ltd.

Kapur, Nick (2018). *Japan at the Crossroads: Conflict and Compromise after Anpo.* Cambridge, Massachusetts, and London, England: Harvard University Press.

Kayama, Shigeru (2023). *Godzilla and Godzilla Raids Again.* Minneapolis: University of Minnesota Press.

Kimura, Manabu [Editor] (2022a). *Godzilla, Mothra, and King Ghidorah: Giant Monsters All-Out Attack Completion*. Tokyo: Hobby Japan Co., Ltd.

Kimura, Manabu [Editor] (2022b). *Mothra vs. Godzilla Completion*. Tokyo: Hobby Japan Co., Ltd.

Kimura, Manabu [Editor] (2023). *Ghidorah, the Three-Headed Monster Completion*. Tokyo: Hobby Japan Co., Ltd.

Kingston, Jeff (2014). *Japan in Transformation, 1945-2010* (Second Edition). London and New York: Routledge.

Kinsey, Wayne (2002). *Hammer Films: The Bray Studios Years*. London: Reynolds & Hearn Ltd.

Kohso, Sabu (2024). *Life of Militancy: Japan's Long '68*. https://illwill.com/life-of-militancy [Accessed 14/2/24]

Lu, Sidney Xu (2019). *The Making of Japanese Settler Colonialism: Malthusianism and Trans-Pacific Migration, 1868-1961*. Cambridge: Cambridge University Press.

Marotti, William (2013). *Money, Trains, and Guillotines: Art and Revolution in 1960s Japan*. Durham and London: Duke University Press.

Masafumi, Okazaki (2010). *Chrysanthemum and Christianity: Education and Religion in Occupied Japan, 1945-1952* in Pacific Historical Review, Vol. 79, No. 3, pp. 393-417. University of California Press.

Matsumura, Wendy (2015). *The Limits of Okinawa: Japanese Capitalism, Living Labor, and Theorizations of Community*. Durham and London: Duke University Press.

Matsuoka, Yosuke (1933). *Japan's Case in the Sino-Japanese Dispute*. New York: Japanese Chamber of Commerce of New York, Inc.

Mayumi, Morai & Sand, Jordan (2020). *Kasumigaoka Apartments: The People Evicted Twice for the Tokyo Olympics in City & Society*, Vol. 32, Issue 2, pp. 436-47. American Anthropological Association.

McClain, James L. (2001). *Japan: A Modern History*. New York and London: W. W. Norton & Company.

McKenna, A. T. (2016). *Showman of the Screen: Joseph E. Levine and His Revolutions in Film Promotion*. Lexington: The University Press of Kentucky.

Melber, Takuma (2021). *Pearl Harbor: Japan's Attack and America's Entry into World War II*. Cambridge: Polity Press.

Michelson, Annette [Editor] (1992). *Cinema, Censorship, and the State: The Writings of Nagisa Oshima*. Cambridge, Massachusetts: The MIT Press.

Mirjahangir, Chris (2022). *Ishiro Honda: His Final Interview*. https://www.tohokingdom.com/blog/ishiro-honda-his-final-interview/?fbclid=IwAR2894k4VX8jj_ZFN013zTWmZ0byvUv7oFg0yJr4kuWpS0sny6tVOQG70F4 [Accessed 20/12/22]

Miura, Takashi (2017). *The Buddha in Yoshiwara: Religion and Visual Entertainment in Tokugawa Japan as Seen through Kibyōshi in Japanese Journal of Religious Studies*, Vol. 44, No. 2, pp. 225–54. Nanzan University.

Miyamoto, Yuki (2012). *The Ethics of Commemoration: Religion and Politics in Nanjing, Hiroshima, and Yasukuni in Journal of the American Academy of Religion*, Vol. 80, No. 1, pp. 34–64. Oxford University Press.

Morris-Suzuki, Tessa (2021). *The "Comfort Women" Issue, Freedom of Speech, and Academic Integrity: A Study Aid in The Asia-Pacific Journal: Japan Focus*, Vol. 19, Issue 5, No. 2.

Nakajima, Haruo (2010). *Monster Life*. Tokyo: Yosensha Co., Ltd.

Nakamura, Satsohi & Hazawa, Masato (2014). *Godzilla Toho Champion Festival Perfection*. Tokyo: Kadokawa Books, Co., Ltd.

Nakamura, Shinichiro, Fukunaga, Takehiko, & Hotta, Yoshie (1994). *The Luminous Faires and Mothra*. Tokyo: Chikuba Shobo.

Nakano, Teruyoshi & Someya, Katsuji (2007). *Teruyoshi Nakano the SFX Director*. Tokyo: Wides Shuppan.

Noriega, Chon (1987). *Godzilla and the Japanese Nightmare: When "Them!" is U.S. in Cinema Journal*, Vol. 27, No. 1, pp. 63–77. University of Texas Press on behalf of the Society for Cinema and Media Studies.

Okita, Saburo (1951). *Japan's Economy and the Korean War in Far Eastern Survey*, Vol. 20, No. 14, pp. 141–44. Institute of Pacific Relations.

Ono, Koichiro & Iwahata, Toshiaki [Editors] (2023). *Godzilla & Toho Special Effects Films Official Mook Vol. 06: Ghidorah, the Three-Headed Monster*. Tokyo: Kodansha Ltd.

Ono, Sokyo (1962). *Shinto: The Kami Way*. North Clarendon: Tuttle Publishing.

Packard, George R. (1966). *Protest in Tokyo: The Security Treaty Crisis of 1960*. Rahway, New Jersey: Princeton University Press.

Packard, George R. (1987). *The Coming U.S.-Japan Crisis in Foreign Affairs*, Vol. 66, No. 2, pp. 348–67. Council on Foreign Relations.

Philips, Alastair & Stringer, Julian (2007). *Japanese Cinema: Texts and Contexts*. London and New York: Routledge.

Pink, Sidney (1989). *So You Want to Make Movies: My Life as an Independent Film Producer*. Florida: Pineapple Press, Inc.

Ragone, August (2007). *Eiji Tsuburaya: Master of Monsters*. San Francisco: Chronicle Books.

Rawle, Steven (2022). *Transnational Kaiju: Exploitation, Globalisation, and Cult Monster Movies*. Edinburgh: Edinburgh University Press.

Reider, Noriko T. (2003). *Transformation of the Oni: From the Frightening and Diabolical to the Cute and Sexy in Asian Folklore Studies*, Vol. 62, pp. 133–57. Miami University.

Rhoads, Sean & McCorkle, Brooke (2018). *Japan's Green Monsters: Environmental Commentary in Kaiju Cinema*. Jefferson, North Carolina, and London: McFarland & Company, Inc., Publishers.

Richie, Donald (1996). *The Films of Akira Kurosawa* (Third Expanded Edition). Berkeley, Los Angeles, and London: University of California Press.

Ryfle, Steve (1998). *Japan's Favorite Mon-Star: The Unauthorized Biography of "The Big G"*. Toronto, Ontario, Canada: ECW Press.

Ryfle, Steve & Godziszewski, Ed (2017). *Ishiro Honda: A Life in Film from Godzilla to Kurosawa*. Middletown, CT: Wesleyan University Press.

Ryu, Yongwook (2007). *The Yasukuni Controversy: Divergent Perspectives from the Japanese Political Elite in Asian Survey*, Vol. 47, No. 5, pp. 705–26. University of California Press.

Sakamoto, Kazuya (2001). *Advancing the Japan-US Alliance* in *Japan Quarterly*, Vol. 48, Issue 2, pp. 18–24. Tokyo: Asahi Shimbun.

Schieder, Chelsea Szendi (2021). *The History the Japanese Government is Trying to Erase*. https://www.thenation.com/article/world/ramseyer-comfort-women-japan-nationalism/ [Accessed: 23/08/23]

Shapiro, Jerome F. (2002). *Atomic Bomb Cinema*. London and New York: Routledge.

Sharp, Jasper (2011). *Historical Dictionary of Japanese Cinema*. Plymouth, UK: Scarecrow Press, Inc.

Shibata, Yuko (2018). *Producing Hiroshima and Nagasaki: Literature, Film, and Transnational Politics*. Honolulu: University of Hawai'i Press.

Shibuichi, Daiki (2005). *The Yasukuni Shrine Dispute and the Politics of Identity in Japan: Why All the Fuss?* in *Asian Survey*, Vol. 45, No. 2, pp. 197–215. University of California Press.

Sims, Richard (2001). *Japanese Political History since the Meiji Renovation 1868–2000*. New York: Palgrave.

Singh, Bhubhindar (2002). *Asean's Perceptions of Japan: Change and Continuity* in *Asian Survey*, Vol. 42, No. 2, pp. 276–96. University of California Press.

Sobchack, Vivian (2004). *Screening Space: The American Science Fiction Film*. New Brunswick, New Jersey, and London: Rutgers University Press.

Southard, Susan (2016). *Nagasaki: Life after Nuclear War*. New York: Penguin.

Takaki, Junzo [Editor] (1998). *Godzilla Chronicles*. Tokyo, Japan: Sony Magazines Inc.

Tamamoto, Masaru (2001). *A Land without Patriots: The Yasukuni Controversy and Japanese Nationalism* in *World Policy Journal*, Vol. 18, No. 3, pp. 33–40. Duke University Press.

Tanaka, Tomoyuki [Supervisor] (1983). *Complete History of Toho SFX Movies*. Tokyo, Japan: Seioh Printing Co., Ltd.

Tanaka, Tomoyuki [Supervisor] (1991). *Encyclopedia of Godzilla: Godzilla vs King Ghidorah Edition*. Japan: Gakushu Kenkyusha Ltd.

Tanaka, Yuki (2002). *Japan's Comfort Women: Sexual Slavery and Prostitution during World War II and the US Occupation*. London and New York: Routledge.

Tanobe, Naoto [Editor] (2011a). *Toho SFX Actresses Encyclopedia*. Tokyo: Yosensha Co., Ltd.

Tanobe, Naoto [Editor] (2011b). *Movie Hidden Treasure, Mothra Movie Encyclopedia*. Tokyo: Yosensha Co., Ltd.

Tsutsui, William (2004). *Godzilla on my Mind*. New York and England: Palgrave MacMillan.

Tsutsui, William & Ito, Michiko [Editors] (2006). *In Godzilla's Footsteps: Japanese Pop Culture Icons on the Global Stage*. New York: Palgrave.

Uemura, Hideaki (2003). *The Colonial Annexation of Okinawa and the Logic of International Law: The Formation of an 'Indigenous People' in East Asia* in *Japanese Studies*, Vol. 23, No.2, pp. 107–24. Carfax Publishing.

Walden, Victoria Grace (2016). *Studying Hammer Horror*. Leighton Buzzard: Auteur Publishing.

Walker, Johnny [Editor] (2021). *Hammer and Beyond: The British Horror Film*. Manchester: Manchester University Press.

Weglyn, Michi (2003). *Years of Infamy: The Untold Story of America's Concentration Camps* (Third Printing). Seattle and London: University of Washington Press.

Weisgall, Jonathon M. (1994). *Operation Crossroads: The Atomic Tests at Bikini Atoll*. Annapolis, Maryland: Naval Institute Press.

Wilson, Sandra (2012). *Exhibiting a New Japan: the Tokyo Olympics of 1964 and Expo '70 in Osaka* in *Historical Research*, Vol. 85, No. 227, pp. 159–78. Institute of Historical Research, School of Advanced Study, University of London.

Yasumaro, O No (2014). *The Kojiki: An Account of Ancient Matters*. New York: Columbia University Press.

Yomota, Inuhiko (2019). *What Is Japanese Cinema? A History*. New York: Columbia University Press.

Yoshimi, Shunya (2019). *1964 Tokyo Olympics as Post-War* in *International Journal of Japanese Sociology*, No. 28, pp. 80–95. The Japan Sociological Society.

Film Scripts

Sekizawa, Shinichi (1964, reprinted 2016). *Ghidorah, the Three-Headed Monster* [Third Draft]. Tokyo: Gakken Plus Co., Ltd.

Theatrical Programme Booklets

Ghidorah, the Three-Headed Monster (December 1964). Toho.

King Kong vs. Godzilla (August 1962). Toho.

Terror of Mechagodzilla (March 1975). Toho.

Documentaries

Bringing Godzilla Down to Size: The Art of Japanese Special Effects (2007). Dir. Norman England. Classic Media.

Godzilla's 60th Anniversary: The Amazing World of Japanese Special Effects (2014). Dir. Toshifumi Shimizu. NHK World TV.

Godzilla King of the Monsters! (1998). BBC.

It Conquered Hollywood! The Story of American International Pictures (2001). Dir. Eamon Harrington & John Watkin. American Movie Classics.

DVD Special Features

Audio commentary by David Kalat (2007). *Ghidorah, the Three-Headed Monster* [DVD]. Classic Media.

Audio commentary by Steve Ryfle & Ed Godziszewski (2009). *Mothra*, Icons of Sci-Fi: Toho Collection [DVD]. Sony.

Interview with Japanese film-critic Tadao Sato (2011). *Godzilla* [DVD]. Criterion Collection.

Music Records

Koseki, Yuji (1984). *Mothra* [Vinyl Record]. Japan: King Record Co. Ltd.

Newspapers and Periodicals

Anon. (1953). '"New Era" Pix Under Attack: No "Salvation" for Us: Starr', *Weekly Variety*, 3 June, pp. 3 & 18.

Anon. (1953). 'Indie Ops' "Go Slow" on Sound: Wait for Costs to Come Down', *Weekly Variety*, 3 June, pp. 7 & 16.

Anon. (1956). 'When it Comes to Beasts !! We Got 'Em !!', *Weekly Variety*, 4 April, p. 21.

Anon. (1956). 'The Age of Anxiety Lives On – And On', *Charlotte News*, 7 July, p. 4.

Ghidorah, the Three-Headed Monster

Anon. (1957). 'DCA Distributor of King Bros'. "Rodan"', *Daily Variety*, 20 September, p. 4.

Anon. (1957). 'Lavish Color Featured in "Rodan" Here', *Galveston Daily News*, 12 November, p. 2.

Anon. (1958). 'Goldman, Schreibman Acquire "Mysterians"', *Daily Variety*, 23 January, p. 2.

Anon. (1958). 'Jap "Rodan", Wilcox's "Battle Hell" Backed by $80,000 DCA Budget', *Weekly Variety*, 19 March, p. 19.

Anon. (1958). 'Television Spots Hypo "Rodan" to Record Boxoffice', *Film Bulletin*, 14 April, p. 24.

Anon. (1958). 'Soundtrack', *Weekly Variety*, 17 September, p. 16.

Anon. (1959). 'Outside-Japan Rights to "H-Man" for Col', *Weekly Variety*, 21 January, p. 28.

Anon. (1959). 'Metro "Mysterians" Sci-Fi from Nippon', *Weekly Variety*, 25 February, p 15.

Anon. (1959). 'Col. Sends "H-Man" Trailer on 8-State Promotional Tour', *Film Bulletin*, 22 June, p. 19.

Anon. (1965). 'Can't Bank "Good Reviews"; Reade-Sterling Takes Emphasis off Arty Pics', *Daily Variety*, 10 September, p. 4.

Anon. (1965). 'Bettered Outlook at Continental Co.', *Weekly Variety*, 3 November, pp. 3 & 21.

Anon. (1965). 'Pasolini's "St. Matthew" for Reade; New Range of Products Ups Quarter', *Weekly Variety*, 24 November, p. 7.

Anon. (1966). '"Ghidrah" In Final 4 Days at the Chief', *Colorado Springs Gazette-Telegraph*, 22 January, p. 2.

Anon. (1966). 'Key Takers for New Reade Pkg.', Weekly Variety, 16 November, p. 30.

B. E. (1956). 'Orpheum's Film Called Thriller', *Spokane Chronicle*, 12 July, p. 12.

Bower, Helen (1957). 'Science Fiction Has an Oriental Twist', *Detroit Free Press*, 4 December, p. 25.

Bustin, John (1956). 'Show World', *Austin American-Statesman*, 2 August, p. 32.

Cedrone jr, Louis R. (1965). 'A Monster Mash in Japan', *Evening Sun*, 14 December, p. 18.

Cook, Louis (1965). 'At the Movies: Monsters – Really Big; Britain's Merry Rotter', *Detroit Free Press*, 22 October, p. 23.

Gilb. (1956). 'Film Reviews: Godzilla King of the Monsters', *Weekly Variety*, 25 April, p. 6.

Guarino, Ann (1965). 'Movies: Non-Swivelling Elvis Plays Sheik, Monster Film on Double Bill', *Daily News*, 16 December, p. 96.

Hall, John (1956). 'Ramon Cops Split Nod Over Vejar at Olympic', *Mirror News*, 25 July, p. 29.

Jameson, Sam (1985). 'Nakasone's Visit to Wartime Shrine Criticized', *Los Angeles Times*, 16 August.

Jampel, Dave (1959). 'Japanese Arters Wow Critics, But Horror Films Get Coin', *Weekly Variety*, 15 April, p. 46.

Robe (1965). 'Film Reviews: Ghidrah, the Three-Headed Monster', *Daily Variety*, 5 October, p. 6.

Roderick, John (1974). 'News Analysis: Japan Not Loved in SE Asia', *Oregonian*, 17 January, p. 2.

Skolsky, Sidney (1958). 'Hollywood is my Beat: The Mail Bag: Your Column', *Citizen-News*, 4 July, p. 5.

Tubbs, Helen McGill (1951). 'Rome', *Weekly Variety*, 3 October, p. 73.

Wolf, William (1966). 'Lost $1.2 Million in '64, Reade Says Firm Now Back in Black', *Asbury Park Press*, 2 January, p. 17.

Index

American International Pictures (AIP)...91–92, 103, 107
Arikawa, Sadamasa 49
Arkoff, Samuel Z. 90–92
Attack of the Crab Monsters (1957).....91, 96
Atragon (1963) 32–33, 47, 81–82, 116

Baragon 116, 118, 132–33
Beast from 20,000 Fathoms, The (1953)..21, 95–96
Britain... 109–12
bullet train *see* Shinkansen

Champion Festival 8, 60–61, 118
China 12, 17, 28, 120–21, 130, 132
Continental Distributing... 89, 99–100, 103–07
Crazy Cats, The 58–59

Frankenstein vs. Baragon (1965) 109, 116–17

Godzilla (character) 20, 22–25, 29–30, 35–37, 49, 51, 57, 63, 68–75, 80–85, 87–88, 101–02, 106, 115, 119, 123, 126–27, 132–33, 135–38
Godzilla (series)
  Godzilla (1954).................... 7, 18–25, 28, 37
  Godzilla Raids Again (1955)....25–26, 42, 51
  Godzilla, King of the Monsters! (1956).........92–97, 99, 109
  King Kong vs. Godzilla (1962)......34–37, 40, 59–60, 70, 75, 84, 115, 117, 122
  Mothra vs. Godzilla (1964).............8, 36–37, 40–41, 46, 51–52, 58, 60, 63, 68–69, 74, 80–81, 84, 103, 115
  Ghidorah, the Three-Headed Monster (1964) 7–11, 25, 37, 39–61, 63, 69–88, 89, 99–107, 115–18, 120, 122, 128, 135–38
  Invasion of Astro-Monster (1965)...59, 107, 109, 120–23, 134–35
  Ebirah, Horror of the Deep (1966) ...59, 107
  Son of Godzilla (1967)...............107, 134–36
  Destroy All Monsters (1968)..107, 116, 122
  Godzilla vs. Gigan (1972) 122
  Godzilla vs. Mechagodzilla (1974) 119
  Terror of Mechagodzilla (1975)........57, 119, 123, 135
  Return of Godzilla, The (1984)..........42, 123
  Godzilla vs. King Ghidorah (1991)......... 119, 123–28, 134, 136
  Godzilla vs. Mothra (1992)..........46, 128–29
  Godzilla vs. Mechagodzilla (1993) 136
  Godzilla vs. SpaceGodzilla (1994) 136
  Godzilla vs. Destoroyah (1995) 119, 136
  Godzilla x Megaguirus (2000)................. 134
  Godzilla, Mothra, and King Ghidorah: Giant Monsters All-Out Attack (2001)............. 119, 130–34
  Godzilla: Final Wars (2004) 119
  Godzilla (2014)................................119, 136
  Godzilla: The Planet Eater (2018)........... 119
  Godzilla: King of the Monsters (2019).. 119, 129

Hammer Films
  American influence 110–13

Curse of Frankenstein, The (1957) ... 110-11
Dracula (1958) 110-11
genre placement by Japanese film critics
see kaiki eiga
Mummy, The (1959) 112
Quatermass Xperiment, The (1955) 110
Hibakusha 28-29
Hirohito, Emperor 12, 14-17, 76
Hirose, Shoichi 48, 137
Hiroshima ... 13, 19, 25, 28-29, 76, 78-79, 81
H-Man, The (1958) 28-29, 40
Hollywood 8, 89-91, 95, 99, 107-08, 110-12
Honda, Ishiro 7-8, 19-21, 24, 26-28, 30, 32-33, 35, 40-41, 45, 54, 57-61, 67, 73, 82-83, 85, 103, 106-07, 109, 122
Hoshi, Yuriko 9, 46, 68

Ifukube, Akira 25, 30, 97, 101-02, 116-17, 126, 136
Iizuka, Sadao 52-57
Ikeda, Hayato 36, 77
Imperial Japan
   colonial aggression 11-12, 15, 27-28, 77, 87, 120-21, 126-27, 130-31
   denial of war crimes 132
   sexual violence 27, 132
Inoue, Yasuyuki 54-57
Irresponsibility of the Great Edo (1964) 58
It Came from Beneath the Sea (1955) 96
Ito, Emi & Yumi 46
Ito, Hisaya 47
Ito, Jerry 32, 63

Japan Bashing 123-26

kaiki eiga 21
Kamei, Fumio 16-17
Kanba, Michiko 31, 79
Kaneko, Shusuke 119, 132-34
Kay, Richard 92-94
Kimura, Takeshi 30, 32
King Ghidorah 7-8, 10, 42-44, 48-50, 52-54, 70-71, 73-74, 81-85, 87-88, 101, 115, 118-20, 122-23, 125-29, 132, 134-35, 137-38
King Kong (1933) 21
King Kong Escapes (1967) 60, 116
Kishi, Nobusuke 27-28, 31, 36, 77-78, 126, 133
Koizumi, Hiroshi 9, 25, 40-42, 63, 68
Koizumi, Junichiro 130-33
Kojiki 85-88
Korea 11, 17, 35, 125, 130-31
Kurosawa, Akira 41, 47, 78, 94, 98, 100

Levine, Joseph E. 92-96, 99, 104
localisation, American 89, 92-94, 97, 100-03, 107-13, 117, 138
lost decade, Japan's 127, 130
Lucky Dragon No. 5 .... 19-20, 28
Luminous Fairies and Mothra, The 32, 64-67

Mabuchi, Kaoru *see* Takeshi Kimura
MacArthur, General Douglas 14-15, 17
Manda 116
Matango (1963) 79-80
miniature effects 54-57
Mirrorman (1971-72) 60
Mizuno, Kumi 41

Mothra (1961) ...8, 32–33, 36, 46, 60, 63–70, 80–81, 84, 108, 115
Mothra (character)..............10, 32–33, 36, 39, 41–42, 46, 52, 63–75, 80–84, 106, 115, 119, 128–30, 132–35
Mysterians, The (1957).......26–27, 37, 47, 99

Nagasaki.............................. 13, 19, 28, 81, 93
Nakagawa, Anna 123
Nakagawa, Nobuo 21
Nakajima, Haruo........... 48–49, 51, 59, 71–72, 135, 137
Nakamura, Shinichiro 64–65
Nakano, Teruyoshi 47
Nakasone, Yasuhiro 131
Natsuki, Yosuke...................... 9, 40–41, 43, 58
Nicholson, James H..91
Nihon Shoki see Kojiki
nuclear weapons 13, 19–25, 26–29, 37, 42–43, 63, 68, 80–81, 93, 96, 98, 112, 119, 123, 128

Occupation (US)
  1947 constitution 15–16
  Civil Censorship Detachment (CCD)...........16
  Civil Information & Education Section (CIE) 16–17, 23
  reverse course 17–18
Operation Antlion (1964)..............................58
optical effects *see* Sadao Iizuka
Oshima, Nagisa...79

Paramount ruling................... 89–92, 110, 112
Peanuts, The *see* Emi & Yumi Ito
Pearl Harbor 13, 120–21

Post-war Japan
  economic recovery 17, 36–37, 66, 68, 75–81, 86–87, 137
  environmental damage 36, 123
  Liberal Democratic Party (LDP).... 26–27, 36, 77–78, 130–33
  rehabilitation of war criminals..... 15–17, 24, 27–28, 77–78, 130

Rebirth of Mothra (1996) ...119, 128–30, 134
Reptilicus (1961) 21, 105
Rikidozan 34–35
Rodan (1956).......26, 37, 50, 84, 97–99, 103, 108, 115
Rodan (character) 9–10, 26, 33, 39, 42, 44, 47, 50–51, 63, 70–71, 73–75, 81–84, 97–98, 101–02, 115, 117, 120, 135
Rolisica 32, 63–68, 81

Sato, Eisaku...77
Saperstein, Henry G............................. 107–10
Security Treaty (US-Japan)
  implications of 18, 24, 33, 65–66, 80–81, 133
  protests against 31–32, 34, 65–66, 78–79
  revision of 28, 30–31
  signing of 18
Sekizawa, Shinichi 30, 32–35, 40, 43–44, 58, 63, 65–75, 80, 137
Shinkansen 76–77
Suzuki, Keiko 49–50, 52–53, 137

Tanaka, Tomoyuki 21, 30, 39–40, 47, 58, 64–65
Takarada, Akira................. 20, 41, 46, 68, 120

Tarantula (1955) 96
Tazaki, Jun..32, 41, 58
Tezuka, Osamu.. 48, 60
Three Sacred Treasures, the....................86-87
Toei..................................... 39, 47, 60, 88, 118
Tokyo Olympics ... 7-8, 37, 46, 75-80, 84, 137
Tsuburaya, Eiji.........15, 21, 30, 36, 40, 48-49, 50, 52-57, 72, 98, 106, 137-38
Tsuchiya, Yoshio 47, 120, 123

Ultraman
   1966-67 series 60, 118
   Feature Monster Movie: Ultraman (1967) 60
   franchise... 118-19
   Return of Ultraman (1971-72).............60-61
United Productions of America (UPA)...... 107, 109

Universal
   Abbott and Costello meet Frankenstein (1948) 116
   crossovers 116-17
   Dracula (1931)....................................96, 116
   Frankenstein (1931) 96, 111, 116-17
   Frankenstein Meets the Wolf Man (1943) 111
   involvement in overseas filmmaking........99

Walter Reade company, the 89, 99-100, 103, 107, 109
Wakabayashi, Akiko......................9, 40-41, 45

Yamata-no-Orochi....................... 48-49, 85-88
Yasukuni Shrine.............................130-32, 134

Zone Fighter (1973) 119

www.ingramcontent.com/pod-product-compliance
Lightning Source LLC
Chambersburg PA
CBHW061452300426
44114CB00014B/1946